Games + Activities + Projects

Bringing Math Home

A Parent's Guide to Elementary School Math

SUZANNE L. CHURCHMAN

Zephyr Press

Chicago

Library of Congress Cataloging-in-Publication Data

Churchman, Suzanne L.
  Bringing math home : a parent's guide to elementary school math : games, activities, projects / Suzanne L. Churchman.
      p. cm.
  Includes bibliographical references and index.
  ISBN-13: 978-1-56976-203-5
  ISBN-10: 1-56976-203-1
1. Mathematics–Study and teaching (Elementary) 2. Mathematics–Problems, exercises, etc. 3. Mathematical recreations. I. Title.
  QA135.6.C53 2006
  375.7–dc22

                                                    2006008027

To R. J. Price
An outstanding principal and instructional leader

Cover and interior design: Monica Baziuk

© 2006 by Suzanne L. Churchman
All rights reserved
Published by Zephyr Press
An imprint of Chicago Review Press, Incorporated
814 North Franklin Street
Chicago, Illinois 60610
ISBN-13: 978-1-56976-203-5
ISBN-10: 1-56976-203-1
Printed in the United States of America

Acknowledgments

I want to give heartfelt thanks to the following:

Bill, my husband, for all the hours of reading, and for his expertise in how to put my ideas down on paper.

My daughter, Michelle, for all the formatting and editing of the manuscript. Her knowledge in these areas was invaluable to the completion of this book.

Becky Medley, for her advice and materials in all things relating to the primary grades, as well as her many years of friendship.

Robynn Clairday, my agent and friend, for her unwavering belief and support.

And my deepest gratitude to R. J. Price, for teaching me how to be a *real* teacher.

This book would not have been possible without the support of the great people at Zephyr Press: my editors Jerome Pohlen and Lisa Rosenthal and their hardworking support team Allison Felus, Production editor, Gerilee Hundt, managing editor, and Monica Baziuk, designer.

Contents

Introduction

From birth to age five you, as a parent, are your offspring's primary mentor. Then, this relationship abruptly changes. Your child goes off to school, and he or she is no longer just *your* baby. You are embarking on one of life's most important quests: the formal education of your child. Even though you have handed off your child's formal learning to someone else, you still have a large part to play. Just as a child's reading ability is affected by how often he or she is read to and by whether reading is a common activity at home, a child's math skills are also greatly enhanced by using math during everyday activities. Parents can provide these experiences.

Perhaps you have fond memories of your own early years in school, when you were learning to write your name, say the alphabet, and count to 100. But wait a minute! School no longer looks like you remember it. You might find yourself saying, "We never had any math like this when I was in school." You might worry how you can assist your child if you don't even understand what's being taught—especially when your child has progressed to the upper elementary years, when the subject matter becomes more difficult. This book will shed some light on the new methods and terminology being used and simplify the confusion caused by these ongoing changes.

In the last 15 to 20 years, elementary mathematics has changed drastically, to encompass much more than simple arithmetic. From the 1940s through the '60s, mathematics in the elementary grades was based on the factory model. During this period, a large segment of the labor force worked on the assembly line. The math needed for this work was basic: addition, subtraction, multiplication, and division. The needs of the business community were reflected in school curriculum.

But beginning in the 1970s, and continuing up through the present, our economic base has gradually shifted from manufacturing to service-related jobs. The manufacturing tasks once done by human labor are now completed by robots, with humans in charge of the machinery. While everyone needs to understand arithmetic, employees no longer need to rely on computational skills. That now falls to the realm of calculators and computers. Prospective workers now need higher-level thinking skills to meet the demands of industry and service-related occupations.

In response, schools have changed, too. As in the past, schools become responsible for preparing the nation's children to become productive members of society. Schools prepare kids to find jobs, and they must coordinate with business to do so. The emphasis has shifted to a much broader understanding of mathematical concepts that promote problem-solving abilities in our youth.

Since 1920 the National Council of Teachers of Mathematics (NCTM) has been dedicated to improving mathematics education for our nation's schools, from pre-kindergarten through 12th grade. Its goal is to monitor our society's economic needs, to keep us competitive with the world's other leading industrial nations, and to research the methods needed to teach those skills, ensuring the highest quality of math education. This nonprofit, nonpartisan organization has developed a set of standards that are used nationwide. Most states and school districts use these standards as the framework for their mathematics curriculum. Textbook publishers often include NCTM standards to show educators that the math texts they distribute are research based and use the latest thinking.

This book will discuss the 10 NCTM-recommended standard areas of mathematics. The first five—Numbers and Operations, Algebra, Geometry, Measurement, and Data Analysis and Probability—are called the Content Standards, since they contain the knowledge or facts needed for mathematics. (Yes, algebra, geometry, and data analysis are taught beginning in kindergarten now.) The last five—Problem Solving, Reasoning and Proof, Communication, Connections, and Representations—are called the Process Standards. These standards tell students "how to do" mathematics.

While at first glance the standards and expectations for elementary school mathematics may seem like a foreign language, don't panic and throw up your hands. It's not as difficult as it sounds. Many of the objectives that are taught are things that you may already be doing with your child as everyday events, such as having your child help when you cook (which teaches fractions and patterns) or teaching him or her to tell time. The most important part of teaching mathematics is to make it relevant to your child—to give it meaning. This is where you can have a huge impact. Doing mathematics in meaningful activities makes it real to your son or daughter.

Since the passage of the No Child Left Behind Act in 2001, schools have been pushed into practicing and drilling vast amounts of material in order for students to pass multiple-choice standardized tests. Due to the emphasis on test results imposed by this act, schools are often left with little time for teaching application and meaning. By providing the everyday experiences that show how mathematics works in the real world, parents can pick up the slack and contribute to their child's education.

How to Use
This Book

This book is a collection of fun and meaningful games, activities, discussions, and projects you can do at home that will help teach the NCTM standards. Each of the first five chapters is based on the NCTM Content Standards. Different skills are expected for primary and upper grade students. Therefore, each chapter is divided into a section for pre-kindergarten through second grade skills and a separate section for third through fifth grade skills. The skills for each section are in **boldface type**. Under each skill, you will find specific games, activities, discussions, or projects that will help you teach it.

For many skills, a Literature Connection is also included. The books listed will help reinforce the skill introduced in the activities. Most are wonderful stories that are great for reading but that also have a mathematical element to them. This is a way to teach two subjects at once: reading and math. For the upper grades, many of the books are more specific to mathematics.

The last five chapters discuss the NCTM Process Standards. The skills for these standards are the same throughout the elementary grades. However, specific applications for these standards are also discussed in separate sections for the primary grades and for the upper elementary grades. Since these skills are what children need to do to apply the Content Standards, examples may be given or references may be made to activities already discussed in the Content chapters.

In the back of the book, you will find three sections that will help you with the various activities. There is a glossary of mathematical terms that are used in this book or that you may find in your child's math textbook. Also included is an appendix with many pages that you can photocopy to help with the activities in the book. Finally, there's a bibliography providing additional resources for more information, some of which are geared toward educators and others which are collections of games that can be played either at home or school. The games, activities, and projects in *Bringing Math Home* are mathematically challenging, but they will also be enjoyable family activities.

CONTENT STANDARDS

In today's mathematics curriculum, the label "Content Standards" encompasses the kind of math skills that most commonly come to mind when you think of your standard conception of "math." For example, the standards covered in chapter 1, "Numbers and Operations," include the computation skills of adding, subtracting, multiplying, and dividing, along with how our number system is set up.

You may also think of mathematics as including measurement, an area we use readily in daily life, which also happens to be another Content Standard area. You frequently need to know the length of objects or the dimensions of areas, the number of pounds needed when buying produce or meat, or a measurement of time in order to complete your daily or weekly routines. You are thus very familiar with two Content Standard areas—Number and Operations and Measurement—and are comfortable using them.

However, there are three other Content Standard areas that may seem a little daunting due to their titles: Algebra, Geometry, and Data Analysis and Probability. These areas sound like something you learned in middle or high school. Today, schools explore these areas with even the youngest of students, but at the appropriate level. The study of algebra at the elementary level is actually pre-algebra, and it lays the foundation for formal study in later years. Geometry is the study of shapes and their properties. Likewise, data analysis explores graphing and organizing information and is the forerunner for more intense study of data and statistics in high school.

All five of these Content Standard areas—Numbers and Operations, Algebra, Geometry, Measurement, and Data Analysis and Probability—contain the basic facts and skills of mathematics. They are the tools that open the door for mathematical thinking.

The first five chapters of this book, each based on one of these five Content Standards, are designed to spell out the specific skills that are taught to different age groups in elementary schools. Each skill is clearly stated, and then a discussion clarifies what is expected of a student who is mastering this skill and why it is important. This is followed by a game, activity, discussion, or project that helps teach and give practice using the skill.

The games, activities, discussions, and projects may involve a child and parent or other adult, a small group of children, or a child working alone. Hopefully, you will find that they not only improve your child's mathematical ability, but are also fun and rewarding.

Numbers and Operations

In the past, the standard for Numbers and Operations would have been known as arithmetic. Much of what children need to know in this area remains the same as when you were in school. Students still need to know how our number system is set up; how to add, subtract, multiply, and divide and how to make computations using paper and a pencil, calculators, or just their brains. Students also need to know what each operation means and how to show numbers in a variety of ways.

Skills and Activities for Grades Pre-Kindergarten to 2

The following text breaks down the broad heading of Numbers and Operations into specific skills that children of this age group should know.

> Young children should be able to count, understand what each number represents, and know "how many" there are in sets of objects.

Counting is the basis for everyday adult math skills, which include everything from monitoring finances and scheduling time, to counting calories, to counting the nuts and bolts provided for assembling a child's first bicycle.

Counting not only means being able to recite the numbers in order (1, 2, 3, and so on), but also understanding that there is a one-to-one correspondence between the numbers and the objects they count. Small children often do this by touching or moving each object as they say the number. While many things they are experiencing as new seem obvious to you as an adult, concepts such as discovering that counting objects in a different order results in the same answer are thrilling to a pre-kindergarten or first grade child. While every child has a different level of maturity, most four-year-olds will start out learning to count to five, and the process grows from there.

Another aspect of counting is "skip counting." This refers to counting by twos, fives, tens, or other numbers. Children are taught to do this by "skipping" certain numbers to reach the next one (1, 2, 3, 4, **5**, 6, 7, 8, 9, **10**).

Counting Mania

Materials
You will need a small group of objects that your child can count. Here is a list to get you started, but the possibilities are endless:

Pennies	Books on a shelf
Buttons	Nails
Beans	Paper clips
Chocolate chips (in or out of cookies)	Chairs
Tiles in a floor	Pieces of cereal

Procedure
You and your child should count as many things as you can, as often as you can. The key to counting is practice. Encourage your child to write the total number he or she counts. Your child can do this with a chalkboard, dry erase board, paper, or something kids really like, such as sticky notes.

Nimble Numbers

Materials
You will need index cards, a marker or pen, paper, and a clock or wristwatch for this activity. Number the index cards, choosing an amount appropriate for the age of your child (such as 0–10, 1–20, or 1–100).

Procedure
Place the cards face up in a random pattern. Keep track of the time that it takes for your child to put the cards in numerical order. By doing this often, you can easily see your child's improvement.

Literature Connection

Anno's Counting Book by Mitsumasa Anno
Count! by Denise Fleming
The 329th Friend by Marjorie Weinman Sharmat

> Children of this age group should begin to understand that numerals have different values depending on what place they occupy (their *place value*).

For example, kids should recognize that in the number 365, the 5 means five ones, the 6 means six tens, and the 3 means three hundreds. They also should recognize that in our base-10 number system, each place to the left is 10 times bigger than the one to the right.

What Does a Number Look Like?

Materials
You will need paper, a pencil, and some type of small manipulative, such as toothpicks, beans, or buttons. Make sure you get a large amount of the manipulative you choose. Divide a sheet of paper in half, with "tens" labeled on the left side and "ones" on the right side; your child will use this place value mat to group tens and ones.

Procedure
This exercise shows place value by asking your child to build a number. Ask your child to count out 54 items, first by making five piles of toothpicks (or whatever manipulative you choose) with 10 in each group and placing them on the "tens" part of the mat, and then by placing four more toothpicks on the "ones" side. Encourage the learner to verbalize the amount—for example, "There are 54 toothpicks, or five tens and four ones." Older students can also work out larger numbers this way with *big* containers of beans, toothpicks, and the like. They should then group by hundreds, tens, and ones.

How High or Low Can You Go?

Materials
You will need recording sheets similar to a spreadsheet, pencils, and a die. If your child is in first grade, you may only want to make a recording sheet with two columns for the

ones place and tens place. For a second grade student, you may need to create a spreadsheet that has three or four columns for the ones, tens, hundreds, and one thousands place. Write the names of the places at the top of each column. Be sure to place the ones column the farthest to the right. You should have two or more players for this game.

Procedure

This game gives children practice finding place value. The object is to make the highest number. You or your child should roll the die. Each player writes the number from the die in one of the columns on his or her spreadsheet. Roll the die until every player has filled all the spaces in one line across. For example, if you are playing with three columns, roll the die three times. Each time, the players must decide in which column they will place the rolled number. The person with the highest number earns a point. Set a target score at the beginning of the game. The person who gets to the target score is the winner. You can also play the game by having kids try to make the lowest number.

Calculator Discoveries

Materials

You will need a calculator.

Procedure

Your child can discover much about how our number system works by repeatedly adding 1 on the calculator. Have your child start with 1 + 1 and continue to press " + 1" many times. Your child may observe that the ones place changes each time he or she adds 1, but that the tens place changes much more slowly, and the hundreds even more slowly than the tens. Use questions to help your child discover that the tens change every tenth time and the hundreds every 10 tens. Early calculator training will help put your child at ease using this important tool.

Literature Connection

The King's Commissioners by Aileen Friedman

Students in primary grades should understand how *whole numbers* (0, 1, 2, 3, 4, and so on) relate to one another.

Concepts such as comparing which number is larger or smaller and how numbers that show order (for example, second, ninth, twenty-fifth) are connected to numbers that show amounts (for example, two, nine, twenty-five) are examples of number relationships.

Larger, Smaller

Materials
You will need to make a deck of 52 cards. You can make these from index cards or a similarly heavy paper and a pen or pencil. Your child should be able to make them with a little help. Choose 13 different numbers that are appropriate for the age of your child (for kindergarten, choose 13 numbers between 1 and 20; for first grade, choose numbers between 1 and 100; and so on). You and your child should make four identical cards for each number. You should have two to four players for this game.

Procedure
This game is similar to the card game War. Shuffle the deck of cards. Deal all the cards. Players stack their cards face down in front of them. Each player turns over one card. The player with the largest number on his or her card wins all the cards. If the cards turned over are the same number, then players turn over a second card. Whoever has the larger number for the second turned-over card wins all the cards. Play continues until all the cards have been played. You can also play the game with the smaller number being the target to win. Players should be encouraged to read the numbers aloud for added practice.

Order, Please!

Materials
You can use the same cards used to play Larger, Smaller to reinforce number order.

Procedure
Have your child take the deck and place the number cards in order from least to greatest or from greatest to least. You can add new number cards for further practice.

Variation
To practice how order numbers are related to counting numbers, make an alternate set of cards so that one card has the counting number and another has the order number (for example, one card has 5, while another card has the word *fifth*). Children can then

match up the related cards. Another variation would be to play the game in the next activity, Number Word Concentration.

Literature Connection

Henry the Fourth by Stuart J. Murphy
The Seven Chinese Brothers by Margaret Mahy

> Young students should be able to connect number words and numerals to the amounts that they represent in a variety of ways.

Number Word Concentration

Materials

You can make cards for this game from index cards or even just scraps of paper and a pen or pencil. Make at least 10 sets of cards. A set consists of a numeral and its number word—for example, a card with the numeral 5 and then a card with its number name, *five,* or a drawing of five squares. You can make more sets to increase difficulty. The number of sets you make depends upon the age of your child. Pre-kindergarten and kindergarten children may only need the numbers 0 to 10; first graders explore numbers to 100; and second graders work with three-digit numbers. You should have two or more players for this game.

Procedure

Turn each of the 20 cards face down on the playing surface. Each player turns two cards over to see if he or she makes a match of the numeral and the number word. If they match, the player gets to keep the pair. If they do not match, the player turns the cards face down again. The next player takes his or her turn. Play continues until all cards are gone. The player with the most sets wins.

Literature Connection

Feast for 10 by Cathryn Falwell

Children of this age group should know common *fractions* (½, ⅓, and ¼) and be able to show what they stand for.

Exploring Measuring Cups

Materials
You will need a large, flat pan, such as a plastic dishpan or even a cake pan; measuring cups (with separate cup measurements for ¼, ⅓, ½, and 1 cup); a dry material such as rice, sand, or split peas for measuring; and containers of various sizes.

Procedure
Children love to explore. One way to explore common fractions is by using measuring cups. With a little direction, your child can discover many things about the relationship between the common fractions written on the cups. For example, your child may learn that ¼ is smaller than ½, even though 4 is a bigger number than 2. Your child will also begin to understand that some fractions are equivalent. It takes two of the ¼ cups to fill the ½ cup.

Your child can also try estimation with this activity. Kids will love to measure out the dry ingredients in the pan. Give your child a number of larger containers and let him or her estimate how many half cups or quarter cups it would take to fill it. Then, your child can actually fill it and find the exact answer.

Fractions in the Real World

Materials
You will need any items that you can cut from a whole into fractions. A pie is a good example.

Procedure
Understanding fractions is another concept that takes practice and more practice. Any time a whole object is cut into equal parts, your child could be learning about fractions. Each time you cut a pie, discuss how many pieces there are in the whole pie; then, discuss how many out of that number are eaten (or left). You can cut candy bars into halves, thirds, and fourths, or divide small bags of M&M's into equal parts resulting in two, three, or four groups. This lays the groundwork for how fractions are used with sets of objects. There are countless instances in your daily life when you are using fractions. The key is to discuss these experiences with your child. Remember to use the

math vocabulary when you talk about fractions: *denominator* for the bottom number in a fraction, **numerator** for the top number, and **equivalent fractions** for fractions that represent the same amount.

Cooking

Materials

Choose a favorite recipe and use the listed ingredients; two tasty examples are listed here. For both recipes, you will also need a large mixing bowl, a mixing spoon, measuring cups and spoons, a cookie sheet, and an oven.

Procedure

Children are always motivated to learn when there is something good to eat. Having your child help you cook or bake gives practical experience in the use of fractions. Here are two cookie recipes that use a variety of fractions.

Brownie Oat Cookies

⅔ cup all-purpose flour
⅔ cup sugar
¼ cup cocoa
1 cup quick oats
1 teaspoon baking powder

¼ teaspoon salt
2 egg whites
⅓ cup light corn syrup
1 teaspoon vanilla
Nonstick cooking spray

Preheat the oven to 350 °F (176 °C). In a large bowl, combine the flour, sugar, cocoa, oats, baking powder, and salt. Add the egg whites, corn syrup, and vanilla. Stir until the dry ingredients are moistened. Drop the dough by teaspoonfuls onto a cookie sheet sprayed with nonstick cooking spray. Bake the sheet in the oven for 10 minutes, or until set. Cool the cookies for five minutes on the cookie sheet. This recipe makes about two dozen cookies.

Peanut Butter Cookies

½ cup granulated sugar
½ cup packed brown sugar
½ cup shortening
½ cup peanut butter
1 egg

1¼ cups all-purpose flour
¾ teaspoon baking soda
½ teaspoon baking powder
¼ teaspoon salt

Preheat the oven to 375 °F (190.5 °C). Mix the sugars, shortening, peanut butter, and egg. Stir in the flour, baking soda, baking powder, and salt. Shape the dough into ¾-inch (1.9-cm) balls. Place them 2 inches (5.1 cm) apart on an ungreased cookie sheet. Bake the sheet in the oven for 10 minutes. Cool the cookies slightly before removing them from the sheet. This recipe makes about four to five dozen cookies.

To increase learning about fractions, you may want to use just the ⅓ cup (80 mL) measure for the Brownie Oat Cookies. Children will then see that it takes two of the ⅓ cup to make ⅔ (160 mL), and it takes three of the ⅓ cup to make a whole cup (240 mL). The same could be done with the Peanut Butter Cookie recipe. This time, vary the experience by using only the ¼ cup measure.

Literature Connection

Fraction Action by Loreen Leedy
Gator Pie by Louise Mathews

> **Young children should understand what it actually means to add and subtract whole numbers.**

Children should know that adding is putting groups together, or "joining," and subtraction is finding the difference between two groups, or "taking away." Children should also understand how addition and subtraction are related to each other. The two operations are the opposite of each other and, therefore, if you know an addition fact, you also know its related subtraction fact— for example, $3 + 8 = 11$, thus $11 - 8 = 3$.

Addition and subtraction facts are all around you in your everyday life. For example, books on a shelf might be an opportunity for your child to add or subtract. There are five white books and two red books. How many are there all together? Or, for subtraction, you can change the question to: How many books would be on the shelf if we took four books down? Or, how many books would be left if we took down the red books?

Writing Equations

Materials
You will need small manipulatives (such as beans), paper, and a pencil.

Procedure
Set out the beans (or whatever manipulative you choose) in two groups and have your child write the equivalent equation. For example, if there were six beans in one group and three beans in another group, then the child would write $6 + 3 = 9$. The opposite would be that you write the equation and have your child use the beans to show the problem. You can use these two activities for both addition and subtraction.

Literature Connection

Addition Annie by David Gisler (addition)
The Great Take-Away by Louise Mathews (subtraction)
On the River: An Adding Book by Sheila White Samton (addition)
17 Kings and 42 Elephants by Margaret Mahy (subtraction)

> Primary grade children should understand that multiplication is the same as repeatedly adding the same number, and that division is equal groupings of objects and sharing equally.

Do You Have More Cookies than I Do?

To show how multiplication is like repeated addition, have your child find the total amount of cookies that are in three bags, with five cookies in each bag. Your child can find the answer by writing out "5 + 5 + 5 = 15," which is the same as 3 × 5 = 15.

Show your child that division, in some situations, is really sharing a larger group equally. For instance, if Johnny has 15 cookies and wants to share them with three friends, each friend would receive five cookies. Sharing is something most kids have been doing since preschool. Each time your child has to share a bag of candy with friends, he or she shares equally—"Here's one for you, and one for you, and one for me." Your child has been dividing and didn't know it.

Literature Connection

Amanda Bean's Amazing Dream by Cindy Neuschwander
Bats on Parade by Kathi Appelt
The Doorbell Rang by Pat Hutchins
One Hundred Hungry Ants by Elinor J. Pinczes

> Young children should begin learning and using strategies for doing addition and subtraction computations with whole numbers, including regrouping.

Regrouping is an essential strategy that children learn in the later years of the primary level. Regrouping is what used to be called "carrying" for addition and "borrowing" for subtraction. These skills can be difficult to master, but if students understand why it works, it is much easier. Kids also need to discover concepts such as the fact that numbers can be put in any order to add, but that the same is not true for subtraction. Another important strategy for younger children to understand is that 0 may be added or subtracted from any number and that same number will be the result—for example, 9 + 0 = 9, 7 − 0 = 7.

Computation Roundup

Materials

You will need 10 cards, each with one of the digits 0 through 9 written on it. Each player needs a piece of paper and a pencil and needs to draw a problem form (see below for examples). You should have two or more players for this game.

Procedure

The object of this game is to practice regrouping in addition and subtraction. This game is appropriate for second graders. Players should copy the problem form shown on their paper. After you shuffle the cards, one player draws a card from anywhere in the stack and holds it up for everyone to see. Each player writes the shown digit in one of the short lines on his or her problem form. After a player writes a digit, it cannot be changed. Each player takes a turn shuffling, drawing, and showing a digit until the players have filled all the lines in their problem forms. Players then solve their problems and check their opponents' answers. In case of ties, each player earns a point. For children in third through fifth grade, you can vary this game by changing the problem form to give practice in multiplication, division, decimals, or fractions. The player with the highest answer wins.

$$+ \ \underline{\quad} \ \underline{\quad} \ \underline{\quad}$$

$$= \ \text{(answer)}$$

$$+ \ \underline{\quad} \ \underline{\quad}$$

$$= \ \text{(answer)}$$

$$- \ \underline{\quad} \ \underline{\quad}$$

$$= \ \text{(answer)}$$

Close to the Goal

Materials

You will need one egg carton without any holes in it, two counters (buttons, beans, or the like will work), and lined paper and a pencil for each player. Write the digits 1 through 9 in the bottom of the egg carton sections. You will need to use three numbers twice; any random arrangement will work. Place the two counters in the egg carton. You should have two or more players for this game.

Procedure

This is another game that will help students practice regrouping in addition or subtraction using two-digit numbers. The objective is to reach a set goal (100 for first graders, possibly 300 for second graders, or higher goals for older students). To reach this goal, players must add and subtract cumulatively. The answer to the first problem becomes the first number in the next problem.

Each player will use the lined paper to add or subtract in a column, 10 times. The first player shakes the egg carton and then opens it and tells the other players which digits the two counters landed on. Each player records the two digits as a number on the first line of his or her paper. For example, if the two digits are 5 and 8, the player could record it as 58 or 85. The next player shakes the egg carton and announces the digits covered by the counters. All players then record these digits on the second line of their paper in any order. If the second shake resulted in a 4 and a 6, players must decide on recording either 46 or 64. Each player must then decide if he or she wants to add or subtract the two numbers (58 + 46 or 58 – 46). The players record the answer on the third line down. The answer to this problem will be the first number in the next problem. The next player shakes the egg carton and follows the same steps as on the second shake. Players must use subtraction at least twice. Play continues until shaking the egg carton has generated 11 numbers.

If a player reaches a number that he or she wishes to stay with for the remainder of the game, the player may hold for the rest of the shakes and stay with that number. The winner is the person who is closest to the goal. See the example at right.

If using three-digit numbers, you will need to adjust the game by using three counters.

$$
\begin{array}{r}
58 \\
+\ 46 \\
\hline
104 \\
+\ 29 \\
\hline
133 \\
+\ 36 \\
\hline
169 \\
+\ 95 \\
\hline
264 \\
-\ 79 \\
\hline
185 \\
+\ 34 \\
\hline
219 \\
+\ 92 \\
\hline
311 \\
-\ 85 \\
\hline
226 \\
+\ 38 \\
\hline
264 \\
+\ 39 \\
\hline
303
\end{array}
$$

Literature Connection

The Philharmonic Gets Dressed by Karla Kuskin
Pondlarker by Fred Gwynne

> As always, students should develop speed and accuracy while using the basic addition and subtraction facts.

Flash cards are effective, but drilling with them alone is often boring. Here are other ways to spice up this needed practice.

Ball-Throw Math

Materials

You will need a box that is divided into sections for this game. You can construct it from any sturdy box or, if available, a box used to hold canning jars is ideal. Write the digits 0 through 9 on the inside of each compartment. You will also need two small beanbags or porcupine balls (rubber balls with short, flimsy rubber stubble all around them) as well as paper and a pencil for each player. You should have two or more players for this game.

Procedure

From a designated throwing line, each player throws the two balls or beanbags into the box, where they will each come to rest in a section. If the thrown objects do not go into the box, the child may throw them again until both are in the box. The players may then add, subtract, or multiply numbers of the sections as prearranged. A point is awarded for each correct answer. The first player to earn 10 points wins.

Mathematical Simon Says

Materials

Players need only their heads, hands, and ears. You should have two or more players for this game.

Procedure

This game is played like the original Simon Says, but children not only have to listen to see whether "Simon says" precedes the rest of the statement before doing the action—they also have to solve a math fact. Examples might be, "Simon says, clap the answer to 4 + 9," or, "Tap your head the number of times that equals 5 times 3." As you remember from the original game, the players should not do "Tap your head . . . ," because that statement did not begin with "Simon says."

Jumping Jack Facts

Materials

You will need flash cards appropriate for your child's age level (using addition, subtraction, or multiplication). You can make these from any readable-sized paper, with the facts written on the front in pen or pencil.

Procedure

This is just another way for your child to memorize addition, subtraction, or multiplication facts. For some children, movement is an important factor for learning. They will more easily memorize information if they are in motion. To memorize each fact (for example, 3 + 4 = 7), your child will do jumping jacks. Have your child start with his or her feet together and arms down, the "original position." Pick up a flash card and show your child the fact to be memorized. On the first jump, your child says the first number of the fact (3). Then, your child returns his or her hands and feet to the original position (+). On the second jump, have your child cite the second number (4) and then return to the original position (=). On the final jump, your child cites the answer (7).

Literature Connection

Cats Add Up! by Dianne Ochiltree

> Children should be taught to use a variety of tools (paper and pencil, objects to be counted, a calculator) and methods (mental math, estimation) to complete computations.

As you can see from the previous activities listed, using objects or manipulatives to help with computations is essential for the younger child. Only when they have a firm grasp of the meaning of numbers, addition, and subtraction should you present them with problems alone on paper. As children mature, they should be encouraged to do the same type of adding and subtracting in their heads that they previously did on paper. There are shortcuts and techniques to help with mental math. One such technique, when adding two-digit numbers, is to add the tens first, then the ones, and put the two together. For example, 46 + 39 becomes 40 + 30 = 70 and 6 + 9 = 15, so 70 + 15 = 85.

Give Me a Date

Materials

You will not need any special materials.

Procedure

Have your child see how many addition and subtraction equations he or she can come up with using mental math, with today's date as the answer. As an example, if the date is the 16th, the equations might be 9 + 7, 10 + 6, 25 − 9, and so on.

Purely Mental

Materials

You will need paper and a pencil. Draw a square on a piece of paper and write five numbers, with one inside the square; one to the left of the square; one to the right of the square; one above the square; and one below the square, as shown. You should have two players for this game.

Procedure

To play this game one player says two positions (such as, *above* and *in*) and names an operation (such as *addition*). The other player must say the problem and correctly give its answer using mental math (6 plus 7 equals 13).

```
         7
      ┌─────┐
   3  │  6  │  2
      └─────┘
         4
```

Pondering Estimation and Calculators

For most adults, estimation is the type of math that we use most in our daily lives. Often it is not necessary for us to know an exact number or amount in order to fulfill our daily routines. For example, when grocery shopping, we do not need to know that we have exactly 3¾ cups of flour left in order to make a decision as to whether to buy more. Likewise, we usually round off prices to make a quick estimate of how much that cartful of groceries will cost. Children should be given many opportunities to estimate numbers and quantities—for example, "How many beans are in the sack?" or, "How many toys are in your closet?" There are opportunities for estimation everywhere.

Calculators are another important tool for computation. Yes, children still need to be taught paper and pencil computations, but there is a place for calculators, even with young children. Because adults use this tool so extensively, children need to feel comfortable using it. One place to start would be to use calculators to keep the scores for games. This allows the young child to be mathematically involved, without taking the focus away from the game.

Another valuable use for calculators by small children is when they are doing problem solving. Often, children's thinking abilities for working through problems are at a higher level than their computational level. In this way, you can stimulate their thinking skills without causing the frustration of not knowing a particular computation skill. For example, consider this problem: "Jane has 256 stamps in her stamp collection and her grandpa bought her 17 more. How many stamps does Jane have now?" A first grade student may know that this problem would require addition, but he or she has not mastered regrouping and so would be unable to solve the problem using the paper and pencil method. Doing the problem on a calculator allows that student to be successful at problem solving.

Literature Connection

Mental Math in the Primary Grades by Jack A. Hope, Larry Leutizinger, Barbara J. Reys, and Robert E. Reys

Skills and Activities for Grades 3 to 5

Specific objectives for Numbers and Operations are also outlined for the upper elementary student by the NCTM.

> **Older students should continue their understanding of the place-value structure of the base-10 number system for both whole numbers and decimals.**

Student in grades 3 to 5 should be able to state, for example, that in 254,678.013, the 2 is in the hundred thousands place, with its value being 200,000; the 4 is in thousands place, with its value being 4,000; and the 3 is in thousandths place, with its value being $3/1000$.

What's My Number?

Materials
You will need paper and a pencil. You should have two or more players for this game.

Procedure
This game is similar to Twenty Questions, which you may have played as a child. This time, however, the object is to guess a three-digit number. One player writes a number down on a piece of paper without showing any of the other players. The opponent tries to gather clues about what the number is by asking only yes or no questions. At first,

you may not want to set a limit on the number of questions allowed until your child develops some strategies for discovering the number. Later, you can set limits according to the level of the players. You can vary this game by increasing the number of digits or including decimals.

Number Stumpers

Materials
You will need paper and a pencil. You should have two or more players for this game.

Procedure
This activity is best suited to fifth grade students. They often like the challenge of a riddle.

This activity is the reverse of What's My Number? Have your child think of a number and then write clues that will lead another player to the number. For example, supposing the number 2,345 was the target number, your child might give the following clues:

> It is between 2,000 and 3,000.
> It is a number that would round down to the nearest thousand.
> It has no two digits alike.
> It is a multiple of 5.
> Its digits are consecutive numbers.
> The sum of the digits is 14.

Decimal Battle

Materials
You will need to make a deck of 52 cards with index cards or similar weight paper and a pen or pencil. Using 13 different decimal numbers (for example, 365.13 or 9.246), make four cards for each number. The decimal points should appear in different places so that children will become familiar with tenths, hundredths, and thousandths. The decimals should have from four to six digits. You should have two players for this game.

Procedure
Shuffle the deck. Deal all the cards to the two players. Players stack their cards face down in front of themselves. Both players turn over the top card. The player with the card that has the higher amount wins. If the cards are the same, the players turn over a second card from each stack. The player with the card that is higher then takes all four cards. Play continues until the cards are all played.

Literature Connection

Big Numbers: And Pictures That Show Just How Big They Are! by Edward Packard
Can You Count to a Googol? by Robert E. Wells
How Much Is a Million? by David M. Schwartz

 Students should recognize that numbers can be shown in a variety of ways.

Numbers can be shown in the standard form, such as 278; in word form, such as *two hundred and seventy-eight;* in expanded form, such as 200 + 70 + 8; and in place-value form, such a 2 hundreds, 7 tens, and 8 ones. For some numbers, fractions are another expression of a number, such as 2 being equivalent to ½.

Off to the Races

Materials
You will need a three-minute egg timer or a wristwatch with a second hand to time the rounds. Each player will need paper and pencil. You can have two or more players for this game, although one child can also play alone.

Procedure
Children enjoy the competition found in math races. This race can pit player against player or simply be a competition with a child against him or herself to improve the time. At a signal to start, each player writes as many forms of a given number until the three-minute time limit is up. The player with the most correct forms for the number receives a point. If the child is playing alone, suggest that he or she keep a dated record of the number of forms produced each time. It is motivating for children to see that they are improving with practice.

 Upper grade students should further develop an understanding of fractions.

Children should be able to recognize fractions as parts of wholes or sets of objects and understand that fractions are actually divisions of whole numbers. They should be able to judge the size of fractions through the use of models, pictures, or diagrams.

I Want More

Materials

You will need two dice, one labeled with the numerals 1, 2, 3, 4, 6, and 8. The other die should have the numerals 1, 2, 4, 6, 8, and 12. You can use regular dice for this by writing the appropriate numbers on small pieces of masking tape. Each player should have a piece of paper and a pencil, crayon, or marker. You should have two or more players for this game.

Procedure

This game is a fun way to practice comparing the size of fractions. The first player rolls both dice. The player will use one number as the numerator (top number) of the fraction and the other as the denominator (bottom number). As an example, if the player rolls a 6 and an 8, he or she must decide whether to name it as $6/8$ or $8/6$. After choosing, the player must draw a picture that models the fraction and label it with the fraction. The player can use pies or rectangles that are divided by the denominator, then color in the number of sections that represent the numerator. The second player then does the same. The player who has more gets a point. To extend this game, both players can write an equation or number sentence to show the comparison of the two fractions—for example, $6/8 > 8/12$ or $8/6 < 12/8$ ($6/8$ is greater than $8/12$ or $8/6$ is less than $12/8$). In case of a tie, roll again, and the player with "more" receives two points.

Stick 'Em Up Fractions

Materials

You will need 50 tongue depressors, craft sticks, or Popsicle sticks. On one side of each stick, use a ballpoint pen or permanent marker to write a fraction. You will use each fraction twice. These are the fractions used: $0/2$, $1/2$, $2/2$, $0/3$, $1/3$, $2/3$, $3/3$, $0/4$, $1/4$, $2/4$, $3/4$, $4/4$, $0/12$, $1/12$, $2/12$, $3/12$, $4/12$, $5/12$, $6/12$, $7/12$, $8/12$, $9/12$, $10/12$, $11/12$, and $12/12$. You should have two to four players for this game.

Procedure

This game requires a little work to make, but it should endure many months or years of playing. Place all 50 sticks face down on the playing surface, mixing them up. Without looking, each player draws six sticks. One player says, "Go." All players turn over their sticks and arrange them from least to greatest, with the least being on the left. The player who correctly orders his or her six sticks first wins and receives a point. Return all the sticks to the face down pile, remix, and begin round two. Continue until 10 rounds are played.

Literature Connection

Eating Fractions by Bruce McMillan
The Hershey's Milk Chocolate Bar Fractions Book by Jerry Pallotta

> Older elementary children should recognize and be able to produce other numbers that are equivalent to commonly used fractions, decimals, and per-cents—for example, ¼ = 0.25 = 25 percent.

Picture This!

Materials

Use the Tens Grid or the Hundreds Grid in the Appendix (see pages 203–204) to do the following activities. If you do not have access to a copier, any grid or graph paper will do, as long as it is framed or cut to make a rectangle that has 10 squares across the top and 10 squares down. You will also need a pencil, paper, and crayons or colored markers.

Procedures

Diagrams, drawings, and pictures make it easier for kids to recognize that fractions, decimals, and percentages are equivalent.

Activity 1

Using the Tens Grid, have your child color stripes in a repeating pattern—for instance, a red stripe, an orange stripe, and a polka-dotted stripe. Repeat until the Tens Grid is completely colored. Your child should write a fraction and decimal that show what part of the grid is red, orange, or polka-dotted.

Activity 2

Have your child color a design using different colors on the Hundreds Grid. Your child should write the fraction and decimal for each color.

Activity 3

Have your child draw a picture of the state that you live in on the Hundreds Grid. You and your child should write the fraction, decimal, or percentage of the picture that is colored and not colored.

Activity 4

Using the Hundreds Grid, have your child make a design that is 0.33 green, 0.12 yellow, and 0.45 blue. You and your child should write the fraction for each part. Ask your child to be creative with his or her design, but to fill in only the correct number of squares for each color. Now, your child should write fractions that tell what part of the design is green, yellow, or blue. What fraction is left over, uncolored?

> Students in this age group should begin to explore and investigate numbers less than 0.

Over the Edge

Materials

You will need two dice, both with the numbers 0, 1, 1, 2, 2, and 3. One of the die needs to have the numbers written in red, the other in blue. Again, you can use masking tape to cover the numerals on regular dice. This game is designed for two players. Each player needs a counter and a piece of plain paper to draw his or her playing area.

Procedure

This game is an introduction to positive and negative numbers. Each player should create a playing area. The playing area is a **number line** like the one below:

−7 −6 −5 −4 −3 −2 −1 0 +1 +2 +3 +4 +5 +6 +7.

Each player places his or her counter on zero on a playing area. The red numbered die is used for positive numbers and the blue one is used for negative numbers. The two players take turns. Each player in turn rolls both dice. The players must move their counters to the positive side to reflect the number on the red die and then move toward the negative side to reflect the number on the blue die. Each time it is a player's turn, the player begins from where he or she last stopped. The player who goes "over the edge" on either end is the winner.

> Upper grade children should describe classes of numbers according to the characteristics they possess.

Students should understand definitions for those characteristics such as odd and even numbers, **prime numbers** (whole numbers that have only themselves and 1 as factors) and **composite numbers** (integers that can be divided by other whole numbers besides 1 and themselves), **factors** (numbers that are multiplied together; for example, 2 × 5 = 10—2 and 5), and **multiples** (for example, multiples of 4 are 4, 8, 12, 16, 20, 24, and so on).

Just Ask Me

Materials
You will need a deck of 100 cards made from index cards. Number the cards from 1 to 100 using both the numeral and the number word. Having your child help make the deck gives him or her review and practice in writing and reading number words. Only write on one side of the card. (Be sure to write lightly, or the numbers will show through.) As an alternative, you can use craft sticks instead of the cards. You should have two players for this game.

Procedure
This game has several variations that give practice to the number characteristics already described. Turn the cards or sticks face down. The first player picks a card, not showing his or her opponent. The second player asks, "Is it odd (even)?" If the guess is correct, the second player takes the card or stick. If the guess was incorrect, the first player keeps it. The second player then draws, and the first player guesses. Play continues until all the cards or sticks have been drawn. The player with the most cards or sticks wins.

Variation
Using the same cards or sticks and the same basic rules, you can change the game to practice other number characteristics—for example, multiples and factors, or prime and composite numbers. Questions might sound like: "Is the number a multiple of ___ ?" "Does this number have a factor of ___ ?" or "Is this number prime (composite)?" If these characteristics are new to you, please check the math vocabulary in the Glossary at the back of the book.

Literature Connection
The Number Devil by Hans Magnus Enzensberger

Upper grade students should understand various meanings of multiplication and division.

It is important that students know what each number in an equation represents. In 34 × 16, the learner should recognize that 34 stands for a number of objects and 16 is the number of groups of 34. Students need to relate multiplication to addition, observing that it is really adding the same number a certain number of times: for example, 8 × 6 is the same as 8 + 8 + 8 + 8 + 8 + 8. Just as multiplication is the same as repeated addition, division is the same as repeatedly subtracting a number. For example, 18 divided by 6 is the same as repeatedly subtracting 6 from 18 three times: 18 − 6 = 12, 12 − 6 = 6, 6 − 6 = 0. In other words, 6 has been taken out of 18 three times. Fractions are also a way to show division: ¾ is really 3 divided by 4.

Children also need to understand the effects of multiplying and dividing whole numbers. When whole numbers are multiplied, the **product,** or answer, is larger than either of the numbers that are multiplied. Division of whole numbers results in a smaller number than the number with which you began.

Roll a Rectangular Array

This activity enhances the concepts of multiplication and division by making pictorial representations of both operations. For example, 3 rows of 6 equal a total of 18 squares.

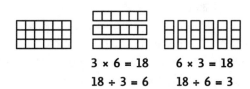

3 × 6 = 18   6 × 3 = 18
18 ÷ 3 = 6   18 ÷ 6 = 3

Materials
You will need two dice, each numbered 1 to 6. Each player will also need crayons, pencils, or markers. The playing field is a piece of graph paper that has at least 12 squares across the top and 12 squares vertically. If the graph paper has more squares than the 12 by 12, you will need to frame the playing field to those dimensions. You may use the centimeter grid paper in the Appendix (see page 205). You should have two or more players for this game.

Procedure
Each player in turn rolls both dice and makes a rectangle using the numbers on the dice as the dimensions. For example, if a player rolls a 3 and a 5, he or she draws a rectangle that is five squares horizontally and three squares high. The player has the option of turning the rectangle so that it has three squares horizontally and is five squares high. The player labels the rectangle with the correct multiplication and division problem, 5 × 3 = 15 and 15 ÷ 3 = 5. He or she could also write the related addition problem,

5 + 5 + 5 = 15. All rectangles must be made within the 12 by 12 playing field, may touch, but not overlap, and may not be drawn inside any other rectangle. Points for scoring are the number of squares within the rectangle that is formed. A player must drop out when he or she cannot make the rectangle he or she has rolled because it will not fit on the playing field. The last player to draw a rectangle receives an extra 10 points. The player with the most accumulated points is the winner.

Variation
For fifth grade or older students, you can increase the difficulty level by using dice with larger numbers. The dice could each have six two-digit numbers. You can change the numbers by taping over 1 through 6 and writing the numbers you wish to use. You will need to use quarter-inch graph paper (see the Appendix, page 206).

I Know What It Costs

Materials
You will need a menu, paper, and a pencil. Often, local restaurants will give out menus at no cost.

Procedure
Have your child figure out the cost of the family eating out. Your child will gain multiplication and addition practice while figuring the cost of each item, as well as the total. To make this a multiplication drill, have your child figure several of the same item. For instance, what would it cost for three of the same sandwich or five of the same soft drink? This not only offers math practice, but it also allows your child to see how expensive it might be for the whole family to eat out.

Literature Connection
Esio Trot by Roald Dahl
One Grain of Rice: A Mathematical Folktale by Demi
A Remainder of One by Elinor J. Pinczes

> **Upper elementary students should recognize and use relationships between operations, such as division being the opposite of multiplication, to solve problems.**

Computation Hangman

Materials

You will only need paper and pencils. You should have two players for this game.

Hangman's Problem Form

```
        65          __ __
    ×   34      ×   __ __
       260          __ __ __
    + 1950          __ __ __ __
      2210
```

Procedure

This game is based on the traditional game of Hangman. The player who is the hangman writes a long addition, subtraction, multiplication, or division problem on one piece of paper, being careful not to show it to the other player. Addition and subtraction problems should not use numbers larger than four digits. Multiplication problems should not use numbers larger than three digits. Division problems should be no larger than two-digit numbers divided into four-digit numbers. The first player should draw a blank problem form on a second piece of paper and show it to his or her opponent.

The second player guesses digits. If they are in the hangman's problem, the hangman writes them on the form as many times as they appear in the problem. If they are incorrect guesses, the hangman draws a part of the hanged man on a third piece of paper. The second player can make seven guesses before the hangman is the winner. The guesser is the winner if he or she gets the problem in less than seven guesses. These are the parts that are drawn for incorrect guesses: head, body, right leg, left leg, right arm, left arm, and face.

Literature Connection

Anno's Mysterious Multiplying Jar by Masaichiro Anno and Mitsumasa Anno

> Older students should understand and use the properties of the four operations (addition, subtraction, multiplication, and division).

The **commutative property** states that the order of numbers does not make a difference in addition or multiplication, but it does in subtraction and division: $6 + 4 = 4 + 6$, but $6 - 4 \neq 4 - 6$.

The **identity property** states that when 0 is added to or subtracted from a number, that number remains the same: $4 + 0 = 4$, $17 - 0 = 17$; or if a number is multiplied by 1: $35 \times 1 = 35$.

The **associative property** states that grouping does not make any difference for addition and multiplication: $(2 \times 3) \times 4 = 2 \times (3 \times 4)$.

The **distributive property** states that the number outside the parenthesis is distributed to each number inside: $5 \times (3 + 4) = (5 \times 3) + (5 \times 4)$.

While you may need to point out and explain these properties to your child, they are not a goal in themselves. As children work with computation more and more, they often discover these properties on their own. The computation games in this section will reinforce the four operation properties.

Extraordinary Equations

Materials
You will need paper and a pencil.

Procedure
Upper grade students enjoy making long, involved equations. It offers practice in using the parentheses and the associative and distributive properties. Choose a target number. Have your child write an equation that equals that targeted number. For example, if the target number is 24, your child might write:

Younger student: $(9 \times 4) - 12 = 24$
Older student: $3 \times (4 \times 3) - 2 \times (2 \times 3) = 24$

If there are two children doing this activity, then they can check each other's equation to see if it is correct and equals the targeted number. To increase difficulty, use larger numbers for the target number.

> Nine- to eleven-year-olds should develop speed and accuracy in adding, subtracting, multiplying, and dividing whole numbers.

Math Fact Bingo

Materials
You will need small cards or pieces of paper on which to write the facts. You will also need a paper bag, which you will use to shake up the cards, and small items, such as beans, to cover the numbers on the card when they are called. You can use regular

Bingo cards for multiplication. However, you may want to make cards with smaller numbers to use with addition, subtraction, or division facts. You need at least three players for this game.

Procedure

Bingo—using addition, subtraction, multiplication, or division facts such as 7 + 8 = 15—is played the same as regular Bingo, but it provides help in memorizing basic facts. The caller shakes the bag, draws, and reads a math fact. The players must figure the answer and cover the number if it appears on their card. The winner is the one who covers five in a row horizontally, vertically, or diagonally. You may also wish to play "Black Out," where all the numbers on a card must be covered in order to win.

Multiplication Concentration

Materials

As in other Concentration games, you need to prepare sets of cards. In this game, the cards should contain a multiplication fact on one card and its product, or answer, on the other.

Procedure

See Number Word Concentration at the beginning of this chapter for the game procedure.

Computation War

Materials

In this form of the game War, you can use a regular deck of playing cards. However, you will only need cards marked King = 0, Ace = 1, 2, 3, 4, 5, 6, 7, 8, 9, and 10. You should have two players for this game.

Procedure

Your child can use this game to practice addition, subtraction, or multiplication. Decide which operation you will be using before play begins. Deal the cards out evenly to the two players. Form a stack, face down, in front of each player. At a given signal, both players turn over two cards. They each, then, apply the operation to the two cards they turned over. The player with the highest score wins that round. You can either tally the rounds, or you can keep the actual answer of the winning pair as a score. Play continues until all the cards have been played. The winner is the player with the most tally marks or, if you are keeping the answers as points, the player with the highest total points wins.

To add difficulty to the game, you can include the other face cards—then, Jack = 11 and Queen = 12.

Literature Connection

The Amazing Pop-Up Multiplication Book by Kate Petty
Divide and Ride by Stuart J. Murphy

> **Upper elementary children should begin to develop and use strategies for estimating the answers of computations using whole numbers, fractions, and decimals and be able to decide whether the answer is reasonable.**

Estimation is one of the math skills that we as adults use the most. Often it is not necessary to have an exact answer in order to make a decision about a particular situation.

Children at this level should be able to determine when it is appropriate to use estimation and when an exact number is required.

Estimation Topics

Materials
You will not need any materials, but you may need various measurement tools to find the exact answers. Refer to the list of topics in the procedure section.

Procedure
Possibilities for estimation are everywhere. In the following list are examples of things that your child may estimate. As an added math activity, your child could also find the exact answer for each to see how close his or her estimates were.

- Length of a piece of string that will go around a basketball
- Total miles (blocks) to school
- Number of seeds in a watermelon
- Weight of an apple as compared to a pumpkin
- Distance in feet from the front door to your child's bedroom
- Number of graham crackers in a box
- Cost of the canned goods on a kitchen shelf

- Number of kernels of unpopped popcorn in 1 cup
- Number of cups of popped popcorn from a ½ cup of popcorn kernels
- Sum of all the heights of members of your family
- Perimeter (in feet) of the living room
- Number of minutes in the month
- Weight of an average-sized banana
- Total amount of change in each family member's pocket (write as a decimal)
- Distance a football can be thrown

Is This Reasonable?

You can include an estimation of computation with any computation problem. Before working the addition, subtraction, multiplication, or division problem, have your child estimate what he or she thinks the answer may be. This not only gives your child practice with estimation, but also will become a check as to whether your child's answer to the computation problem is reasonable.

> **Upper grade students should be able to add and subtract commonly used fractions and decimals.**

Children begin by adding and subtracting fractions with like denominators (for example, $\frac{1}{4} + \frac{2}{4} = \frac{3}{4}$ or $\frac{7}{8} - \frac{3}{8} = \frac{4}{8}$). At the start, it is best to explore the computation of fractions with models or pictures. Children then can visualize why only the numerators are added or subtracted. Denominators are like labels for fractions, simply naming the size of the pieces, but have nothing to do with "how many."

By the time a child is in fifth grade, he or she should be able to compute fractions with unlike denominators. Models and pictures will still help, but the concept of changing fractions to like denominators has to be taught. This is where children's understanding of equivalent fractions and how to form them becomes essential.

Equivalent fractions can be formed by multiplying or dividing the numerator and denominator by the same number (for example, $\frac{2}{4} \times \frac{4}{4} = \frac{8}{16}$ or $\frac{8}{24} \div \frac{8}{8} = \frac{1}{3}$). When the denominators are the same, then it is easy to add or subtract the fractions.

In the Appendix are Fraction Rods for halves, thirds, fourths, sixths, eighths, and twelfths (see pages 209–210). You can use these to help your child visualize fractions.

Tic-Tac-Toe Fractions

Materials

You will need to construct a playing board with the traditional nine squares arranged in a three-by-three grid. In each square, write the answer to a fraction addition or subtraction problem. On separate cards, sticks, or pieces of paper, write the fraction addition or subtraction problems that correspond to the answers on the playing board. Children may also need paper and a pencil with which to work the computations. You should have two players for this game.

Procedure

One player will use O, the other X. The nine squares will contain fractions. The object in this game is to cover three fractions in a row to win. In order to gain the privilege of covering a fraction on the playing board, a player must add or subtract two fractions. For third and fourth grade kids, you would want all the fractions to have the same denominator for both the fractions added and the fractions placed on the playing board. Fifth grade students should be able to work with fractions with unlike denominators. Each player in turn draws a card. The player works the problem using either paper and pencil or mental math and marks his or her symbol (X or O) over the answer on the playing board. The first player to get three in a row horizontally, vertically, or diagonally wins.

Literature Connection

Fraction Fun by David A. Adler

> Older children should be able to choose an appropriate method and tool, including mental computation, estimation, calculators, and paper and a pencil, for computing with whole numbers.

The choice will vary based on the type of problem the student is trying to solve.

The Calculator 100

Materials

You will need a calculator, a pencil, and paper.

Procedure

The purpose of this activity is for your child to become familiar with the keys of the calculator as well as to gain practice in writing equations and problem solving. Your child is to use only certain designated calculator keys, such as 7, 3, +, −, ×, ÷, and =. The challenge is to see how many different equations that equal 100 your child can make on the calculator using only the designated keys. Your child can use the keys more than once in each equation. You can vary the activity can by changing the keys that your child can use. Your child may wish to record each equation on paper in order to be able to make a count of the number of equations made.

Calculator Questions

Materials

You will need a calculator.

Procedure

Here is a list of questions that your child may explore by using the calculator. The way to resolve the problems and the answers are provided in parentheses following each question.

How many years old are you if you have lived 1,000 weeks? (1,000 weeks ÷ 52 weeks per year = 19.2 years.)

Would you rather have 38 quarters or 188 nickels? (38 × $0.25 = $9.50 in quarters; 188 × $0.05 = 9.40 in nickels. The answer is quarters.)

How many different whole numbers will divide 168 without a remainder? (1, 2, 3, 7, and 168. A total of five numbers.)

How many years would it take you to spend $1,000,000 if you spend $30 a day? ($1,000,000 ÷ $30 per day = 33,333 days; 33,333 days ÷ 365 days per year = 91.3 years.)

Find two numbers whose product is between 530 and 550. (Answers will vary; for example, 27 × 20.)

What number times itself has a product of 144? (12.)

What number times itself has a product of 1,024? (32.)

Mental Math Strategies

Mental math is a technique that, as adults, we probably use daily. Children simply need to be encouraged to try to compute the answers to everyday experiences without the aid of paper and a pencil. There are specific strategies that you can teach. The following books describe these strategies. You may be surprised at the strategies you employ yourself on a daily basis. At the time you attended school, they probably were not formally taught. However, as you get older and have more experience in computation, you develop these strategies. Today, children are being introduced to these strategies in school, since it increases their ability to problem solve more quickly and at an earlier age.

Literature Connection

Arithmetricks: 50 Easy Ways to Add, Subtract, Multiply, and Divide Without a Calculator by Edward H. Julius

Calculator Riddles by David A. Adler

Estimate! Calculate! Evaluate! Calculator Activities for the Middle Grades by Marjorie Bloom

Mental Magic: Surefire Tricks to Amaze Your Friends by Martin Gardner

Algebra

Yikes! That dreaded word: *algebra*. In today's schools, the basis for the algebra that you remember from high school is introduced at the elementary level. Maybe if we had all had this early exposure to pre-algebra when we were elementary-aged kids, high school algebra class would not have been the horrendous experience that many of us recall.

Students at the elementary level are basically involved in looking around their world and discovering that patterns exist in everyday experiences. Often, children view it as a game to locate the pattern in colors, shapes, and numbers. This is the basis for algebra—filling in the unknown and finding categorical and sequential groupings. The educator's job is to relate these patterns to math. Research studies have been done evaluating high school students' performance on standardized tests. Those students who have a pattern approach to mathematics scored considerably higher than those with a more traditional approach.

Today's schools also introduce students to symbolic form at the elementary level. In the early grades, unknowns in equations are represented by a box—for example, $9 + \square = 14$. In the middle grades, a letter is substituted for the box—for example, $9 + n = 14$. Students learn to write their own equations to fit the math problem they are trying to solve.

Skills and Activities for Grades Pre-Kindergarten to 2

In pre-kindergarten through grade 2, today's schools introduce and develop algebraic concepts. Children explore these concepts through work with classification, patterns, relations, operations (for example, +, −) with whole numbers, and step-by step processes of all types. While these exercises are algebraic, students at this level do not deal with symbolic notation (such as the use of letters to represent numbers), which is taught in high school. The basis for the algebra that is taught in the lower elementary grades is explained by the following skills.

> **Children in pre-kindergarten through first grade should be able to sort, classify, and order objects by size, number, and other properties (color, shape, and so forth).**

Sorting, classifying, and ordering help students work with patterns, shapes, and other information. Patterns are the way that young children begin to recognize that their world has order, and this recognition helps them begin to organize the world around them. Patterns are a central part of mathematics at this level. Children who understand patterns understand things more quickly, whether it is in math, reading, spelling, or any other learning situation. Seeing patterns means that learners do not have to relearn how to do things each time they come to a similar task.

How's This Like That?

Materials
You will need a variety of pictures; old magazines are an abundant source for this project. You will also need scissors.

Procedure
Have your child cut out many pictures of similar objects. Your child can then sort these pictures according to a specified category or attribute. The following are some suggestions to get your child started:

PICTURE GROUP	CATEGORY OR ATTRIBUTE
Sort by One Attribute	
Children	boy/girl
	smiling/not smiling
	standing/sitting
Animals	pets/not pets
	feathers/no feathers

Sort by Two Attributes	
Vehicles	cars / trucks

Sort by Three Attributes	
Foods	sweet / sour / salty

Variation

A variation of this activity is for you to sort pictures into groups such as boy/girl and have your child come up with the category name.

Mystery Box

Materials

The only materials you will need are a box (a shoe box or similarly sized box will do) and any household object that will fit inside the box.

Procedure

Children love riddles and mysteries. This activity is a favorite because of a child's curiosity to find out what is in the box. Put the object in the box so that your child does not know what it is. He or she can only find out what the mystery object is by asking questions that can be answered by a yes or no.

At first, your child will try to guess the object outright. (For example: "Is it a ball?") Encourage him or her to be a good detective and ask questions that will provide clues. (For example: "Is it round?" or, "Is it red?") Clues for your child to consider are color, size, shape, use, and so on. As your child become mores proficient at this activity, you may want to have a limit on the number of questions asked, as in the game Twenty Questions.

What Color Is Your Button?

Materials

You will need common household objects that are sortable, such as buttons, and a container for them.

Procedure

Put a variety of buttons (or other small objects) in a jar or container. Your child can sort the buttons by the number of holes or by their color, size, or texture. You might also put a group of (safe) kitchen gadgets in a basket or box and ask your child to sort them by use or by the material they are made of. Your child could sort pocket change into different coin denominations. Or, your child can sort a box of random objects by size, shape, or color. Your child can even sort the toys in his or her closet—types, favorites, soft, or hard. Just use your imagination. The idea is for you to give your child a lot of opportunities to sort different types of objects.

Literature Connection

Billy's Button by William Accorsi
Harriet's Halloween Candy by Nancy Carlson
A House Is a House for Me by Mary Ann Hoberman
Is It Red? Is It Yellow? Is It Blue? by Tana Hoban

> **Primary students should recognize, describe, and extend patterns, such as sequences of sounds and shapes or simple numeric patterns, and translate them from one representation to another.**

When working with patterns, children are inherently curious and highly motivated to discover what is going on. It is a thrill to see the proverbial lightbulb turn on when students recognize that they have discovered the key to a pattern. It is important that they are also able to express this pattern in words.

The next step for children is to add on or continue the pattern once they have uncovered it. For instance, if children are working with color patterns, they must find the point at which the pattern begins to repeat—yellow, red, red, green, yellow, red . . . and so on. Children will express it as the yellow-red-red-green pattern. They can then extend the pattern by repeating more of the color sequences.

To translate from one pattern to another means that the same color pattern could be changed to a rhythm pattern. Instead of using colors, the pattern might be clap, stomp, stomp, snap (fingers). Or it could be translated to letters of the alphabet: A, B, B, C.

Magazine Picture Borders

Materials

You will need magazine pictures of like objects, a 6-by-18-inch (15.2-by-45.7-cm) strip of paper, and glue or paste.

Procedure

Using, for instance, the vehicle pictures your child previously sorted, he or she can arrange them in a pattern on a long strip of paper similar to a wallpaper border. Have your child glue them onto the strip in a repeating pattern. That pattern might be: car, car, truck; car, car, truck, or it might be red car, blue car, white car; red car, blue car, white car.

Let's Clap a Rhythm

Materials

You will need no special materials.

Procedure

Rhythm patterns involve clapping, snapping, stomping, patting (head, shoulder, knees, and so on), or other movements that can be done quickly. One person starts a rhythm. For example, clap, snap, clap, stomp; clap, snap, clap, stomp. When your child figures out the pattern, he or she begins the rhythm also. For added practice, ask your child to say the pattern aloud—for example, "Clap, snap, clap, stomp"—as he or she does the rhythm. To practice translating the pattern, your child might want to say, "A, B, A, C."

Variation

It is also fun for two or more children to do echo rhythms. One child does a rhythm pattern once and the other child tries to echo or repeat the rhythm. Then, the children reverse the roles.

Border Pattern Placemats

Materials

You will need a 12-by-18-inch (30.5-by-45.7-cm) sheet of paper, crayons or watercolor markers, cut-out paper shapes or stickers, and glue (if using cut-out shapes).

Procedure

Using a 12-by-18-inch piece of paper or paper of similar size, have your child decorate placemats for the family table. Your child should pick up to four symbols or small pictures (either drawn or cut out) to arrange in a repeating pattern around the four outside edges of the paper. As an example, your child may choose an apple, an orange, and a banana. Your child then repeats this pattern all the way around the edge of the paper and glues it in place (if using cut-out shapes).

This activity is particularly fun to do around the holidays, using gift-wrapping paper. Children will enjoy finding similar holiday symbols, cutting them out, and gluing them in a pattern around the edges of the placemats.

Literature Connection

The Goat in the Rug by Charles L. Blood and Martin Link
The Very Busy Spider by Eric Carle

> Children of this age group should be able to analyze how both repeating and growing patterns are formed.

Repeating patterns may be shapes, numbers, rhythms, sounds, movements, or pictures. An example of a repeating pattern could be:

○○□ ▽; ○○□ ▽ or
2, 5, 3; 2, 5, 3.

Repeating patterns are found all around us in our everyday lives. Just look around your house and you will find patters in wallpaper, upholstery, cloth fabrics, and wrapping paper, to name a few likely examples.

Growing patterns are sometimes called **increasing patterns**. The pattern actually grows instead of just repeating. An example of this type of pattern would be:

A, B, C, AA, BB, CC, AAA, BBB, CCC
or
2, 5, 8, 11, 14.

Hors d'Oeuvres Are in Order

Materials
You will need small wooden skewers or toothpicks and small chunks or pieces of food such as fruit, cheese, or meat.

Procedure
Everyone loves to eat. How about combining food with math? Using wooden skewers, your child can make something delicious and colorful while practicing patterning at the same time. The food choices are yours, but fruit makes an ideal food for skewers. You

should begin a skewer pattern such as strawberry, pineapple, and melon balls. Then, have your child finish filling the skewer, repeating the pattern you have begun. In order to do this, he or she has to analyze what the pattern is and then extend it. Your child can make smaller pattern chains using toothpicks—maybe cheese, olive, cheese, and a chunk of ham or turkey! You start the pattern with one toothpick, and your child builds the rest of the hors d'oeuvres for your social gathering.

Skip Counting

Teaching your child "skip counting" is another way to teach number patterns. When you were a child, this may have been called counting by twos, fives, or tens. Skip counting actually refers to counting by multiples for a certain number. However, at this age level the term *multiple* is not used. Young students are taught to skip certain numbers in order to extend the pattern. For example, if you are skip counting by twos, you skip 1, but say 2; skip 3, but say 4, and so on. Using a chant can be useful: "2, 4, 6, 8, Who do we appreciate?" Children become aware of the pattern of skipping every other number. The pattern for fives would skip four numbers and say the fifth: skip 1, 2, 3, and 4, but say 5.

By the end of second grade, children should be able to "skip count" from memory the twos, fives, and tens. Other numbers give excellent practice in patterns.

Literature Connection

Anno's Magic Seeds by Mitsumasa Anno
The 512 Ants on Sullivan Street by Carol A. Losi

> Children in the lower grades should begin to analyze mathematical situations and represent them using algebraic symbols.

Kindergarten and first grade students spend considerable time acting out addition and subtraction story problems. The teacher begins showing the children how to represent their stories using mathematical symbols—for example, "Three bears were walking in the woods. They met two more bears by the stream. How many bears are there now?" The children will act out being the bears and discover that there are five. The mathematical symbols would, of course, be written "3 + 2 = 5."

Another type of representation that young children do is to make "story boards."

This takes the same type of story as the one about bears, but instead of acting out the story, students make a picture that shows the story. Children will write sentences (with the help of an adult) that tell the bears' story. Then, children (perhaps with adult help) can write the number sentence (3 + 2 = 5) under it. Children will soon see that these mathematical number sentences are a shortcut to the written word and tell the same relationships.

Picture Story Problems

To help your child understand the concepts of addition and subtraction, it is necessary to make the experiences real. One way to do that is to make up stories using numbers.

Materials
Raid the pantry, bringing out the dried beans, macaroni, or other dry ingredients. You will also need plain and lined paper, pencil, crayons, and glue.

Procedure
Allow your child to role-play the following story:

Three penguins were sliding on the ice. Four more penguins waddled up to them and joined them. How many penguins are sliding on the ice now?

Your child will enjoy drawing and coloring a background for the animals. Then, your child needs to be able to "see" those penguins. Have your child use three beans (or whatever manipulative you choose) for the first penguins, and then four more for the ones who waddle up. He or she can glue the beans onto the picture. With your help, have your kindergartener or first grader translate the story into a mathematical equation (3 + 4 = 7). In time, with practice, your primary student will be able to write the equations on his or her own.

You may also wish to have your child write the story in his or her own words. Your child may use an "invented" spelling of words or use pictures for words he or she does not know along with writing words he or she does know. Another option is to have your child tell the story and have you write what he or she says. Then, you and your child can transcribe the words into mathematical symbols. These symbols are new to your child, and so he or she may feel more comfortable with words until you have had more practice together.

For older students, it is equally important for them to be able to visualize story problems using objects. They may not need to draw the picture, but they still benefit from using objects to understand the story. Once they understand, then they can write the equations. You can make the stories more difficult by using larger numbers.

Literature Connection

If You Give a Mouse a Cookie by Laura Joffe Numeroff
One Gorilla by Atsuko Morozumi

> Primary age children should be able to illustrate (draw or make with objects) the general principles and properties of the operations of addition and subtraction. Two of those properties are the commutative property, using specific numbers (3 + 4 is the same as 4 + 3), and the identity property (0 added or subtracted from a number will give you that same number).

Clothespin Addition and Subtraction

Materials
Your will need index cards, clothespins, a pen or marker, paper, and a pencil.

Procedure
Addition and subtraction for young children should be visual, using objects they can manipulate. One way to help your child make the transition from working with objects alone to using symbols is to use index cards with numbers on them and clothespins. Let's say you write the numeral 5 in the center of a card. Your child can explore all the combinations of numbers that add up to five by clipping clothespins to the left and right sides of the card; two clothespins on the left and three clothespins on the right would be one combination that adds to five. Have your child practice writing the equation that the card shows on paper after he or she has completed a combination—in this example, 2 + 3 = 5.

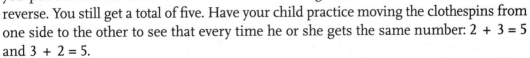

You can also use the cards and clothespins to demonstrate that, when you add, it doesn't make any difference whether you put the two on the left and the three on the right or the reverse. You still get a total of five. Have your child practice moving the clothespins from one side to the other to see that every time he or she gets the same number: 2 + 3 = 5 and 3 + 2 = 5.

This is also a good way to show that if you do not add or subtract anything (0) from a number, you get the number that you started with. For the number 5, your child would put all five clothespins on one side of the card and then not clip (or add) any on the other side, so that the number remains the same. This also can be written in equation form: $5 + 0 = 5$ or $5 - 0 = 5$. You can make cards with all the numbers from 1 through 18.

> As children in this age group use objects, pictures, and verbal presentations to describe what is going on in math stories, they should develop an understanding of the use of symbols to represent those stories. At first, students may invent their own symbols, but as they mature, they should be able to use conventional symbolic notations (such as the use of numerals, $+$, $-$, $<$, $>$, $=$, and so on).

Math Symbol Cookies

Materials
You will need sugar cookie dough, a mixing bowl, a mixing spoon, flour, measuring cups, waxed paper, a rolling pin, cookie sheets, and an oven.

Procedure
Children ages four to seven need to be able to have hands-on experiences with equations. A fun and useful activity is to make numbers and math symbols from cookie dough. Just use your favorite sugar cookie dough recipe, but add an additional ½ to ¾ cup of flour. Then, have your child roll the dough into long, thin strips. (Kids call them snakes.) You may want to roll the snakes out on waxed paper. Form the digits 0, 1, 2, 3, 4, 5, 6, 7, 8, and 9 and the symbols +, −, =, <, and > on cookie sheets. Bake according to the cookie recipe directions. Your child can eat these cookies when you both are finished making equations with them.

Variation
Here is another recipe that you can use if you wish to make numerals and symbols that are more permanent.

Materials
¾ cup all-purpose flour   Mixing spoon
½ cup cornstarch   Measuring cups
½ cup salt   Paint, optional
Warm water   Sealant, optional
Mixing bowl   Paintbrush, optional

Procedure

Mix the flour, cornstarch, and salt together in a bowl. Add warm water until you have formed a stiff dough. Knead the dough until it is pliable. Your child can form the numbers and symbols as he or she did in the cookie dough recipe. These, however, need to dry. When the math symbols are thoroughly dry, your child can paint them and finish them with a sealant.

> Primary students should analyze change in various contexts. Children need to describe change both qualitatively, such as today is warmer than yesterday, and quantitatively, such as a child weighs 10 pounds (4.5 kg) more than last year.

Does Everything Change?

Materials

You will need five items, such as a small plant, food items (such as bread, celery, a potato, or cheese), a metal object (such as a nail in a jar of water), plastic items, or any objects you choose. You will also need paper, pen, and a pencil.

Procedure

Choose five items that your child will monitor for a month, witnessing changes that occur. You and your child should record the changes (or lack of change) on a chart each week for that month. It is best to choose some items that will change dramatically over the month, such as small pieces of food, and some that will not have any observable changes, such as an ordinary ballpoint pen.

You and your child should record information about each item at the beginning of the month, such as measuring the length or height, color, feel, or smell, but *not* taste.

After you have chosen the objects, ask your child to predict what he or she thinks will happen. Will any of the items change color? Will the height, weight, or length change?

Each week, have your child look at the items, discuss changes, and measure and record what was observed.

You will probably need to do the writing, but your child should have plenty of information to give you. Use the sample chart on the next page to get started.

Literature Connection

Slower than a Snail by Anne Schreiber

Chart of Changes

Object	Beginning Observations	How Will It Change?	Week 1	Week 2	Week 3	Week 4
1. Slice of bread	White with brown crust, soft, bendable, good smell	It will dry.				
2. Small green plant	Two leaves, 4 inches (10.2 cm) high	It will get taller.				
3. Gray nail in water	Gray nail, clear water	It will stay the same.				
4. Pencil	Yellow, 7 inches (17.8 cm) long, sharp	It will stay the same.				
5. Celery	Green, leafy, damp, crisp	It will become less damp.				

Skills and Activities for Grades 3 to 5

In grades 3 through 5, all students should understand patterns, their relationships, and their functions (the rule[s] for how a pattern changes).

Children of this age group should identify and build geometric and numeric patterns.

Instead of repeating geometric shapes (for example, square, circle, triangle; square, circle, triangle) like primary children, students in grades 3 through 5 may work with increasing geometric patterns. For example, start with a square with an area of 1 square unit (dimensions 1 by 1), then increase each dimension by one. Now, the square's dimensions are 2 by 2 with an area of 4 square units. The next shape in the pattern would be a 3-by-3 square, with an area of 9 square units. Students would need to analyze the pattern, both for its increasing dimensions and also for the changes in area. You could ask questions such as:

What would be the dimensions of a square that has an area of 144?

What would be the area of a square with the dimensions of 9 by 9?

Numeric patterns also become more complicated. An example might be: 1, 2, 4, 7, 11, ___, ___, ___. Students would then write the rule or describe the changes in the pattern. The rule would be that you are adding 1, then 2, then 3, and so on.

Also included in numeric patterns are everyday patterns, such as time patterns (the numerals on the clock stand for five-minute intervals), money patterns (dimes are counted $.10, $.20, $.30, and $.40), and measurement patterns (2 cups = 1 pint, 2 pints = 1 quart).

Hundreds Board Patterns

A Hundreds Board is just a chart with the numbers from 1 through 100 arranged in rows of 10. You will find one in the Appendix on page 211. Your child can use these boards for many mathematical concepts, but one that is easy and surprisingly interesting is discovering patterns that exist on the board. Here is a list of pattern activities you and your child can do.

Materials
Use small objects, such as scraps of paper, buttons, or beans, and a copy of the Hundreds Board from the Appendix.

Procedure
Have your child cover all the multiples of 2 (2, 4, 6, 8, and so on). Ask your child to describe the pattern on the board.

Now, have your child cover all the multiples of 4 (4, 8, 12, 14, and so on). How is this pattern the same and how is it different?

Have your child cover all the multiples of 3 (3, 6, 9, 12, and so on). Does this pattern look different than the twos pattern?

Have your child experiment with other multiples. Each time, ask your child to describe what the pattern is.

Now, let's get really daring! Have your child cover all the numbers whose digits add up to an odd number. For example, if you add the digits of 34, you get 7 (3 + 4 = 7), which is an odd number. What's the pattern?

Have your child cover all the numbers in which the digit in the ones place is one more than the digit in the tens place (for example, 12, 23, 34, 45, 56, 67, 78, 89).

This is just one way to get your child to explore numeric patterns.

Literature Connection
Mr. Grigg's Work by Cynthia Rylant

> Upper elementary children also should be able to describe patterns verbally or in writing and represent them with tables, graphs, or symbols.

If a child were to describe the pattern for quarters, he or she could say or write that the pattern added 25 for each quarter. The same thing could be represented in a table.

Number of Quarters	1	2	3	4	5	6	7	8
Value of Quarters	$0.25	$0.50	$0.75	$1.00	$1.25	$1.50	$1.75	$2.00

Toothpick Tussle

Materials
You will need a box of toothpicks, paper, and a pencil.

Procedure
Toothpicks make economical building material for making geometric patterns. Your child can use them to show some fascinating increasing patterns. Even more interesting patterns are divulged when your child shows the number of toothpicks used to build the pattern in the form of a table. For example, this toothpick pattern shows a simple growth pattern of squares.

Pattern A	Row	Number of Toothpicks
	1	4
	2	7
	3	10

Notice that the first square requires four toothpicks. Then, as each row increases by one square, you only need three more toothpicks. Children can chart the pattern and predict what will be in Row 8.

Number of Rows	1	2	3	4	5	6	7	8
Number of Toothpicks	4	7	10					

Here are two other toothpick patterns using squares:

Children building these toothpick patterns should be able to compare the three patterns and describe the differences among them. For example, Pattern A increases by one square for each row, but the number of toothpicks only increases by three. In Pattern B, each row also increases by one square, but the number of toothpicks increases by four. Children should be able to tell why this is so. In Pattern C, each row also increases by one square, but the number of toothpicks increases using multiples of

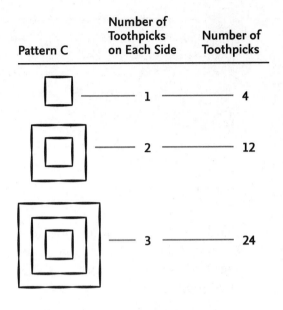

Pattern B	Number of Squares	Number of Toothpicks
	1	4
	2	8
	3	12
	4	16

Pattern C	Number of Toothpicks on Each Side	Number of Toothpicks
	1	4
	2	12
	3	24

four (Row 1 is 4, Row 2 is 4 + 8, Row 3 is 4 + 8 + 12, and Row 4 is 4 + 8 + 12 + 16).

Using the number information from each pattern, your child could show that information on a bar graph. Using the centimeter paper in the Appendix (see page 205), your child can make a separate graph for each of the three squares patterns. On the left side of the graph, she should write the numbers for the number of toothpicks. (Your child may need to number the lines in intervals of two or five in order for there to be room for all the toothpicks that are needed to complete the last row. Just make sure all the graphs are numbered the same way.) Across the bottom, write the number of rows/squares. Your child can then visually compare the increase in the patterns.

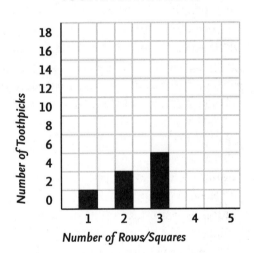

TOOHPICK PATTERN A

Your child can also make triangular patterns by using toothpicks and analyze them by using tables. One such pattern is shown below.

You can ask your child questions such as: How many toothpicks would it take to make a hexagon out of toothpicks—six triangles making the six-sided shape? (Answer: 12.) Or, how many toothpicks would it take if there were 24 triangles arranged in a hexagon? (Answer: 42.)

Literature Connection

The King's Chessboard by David Birch

As previously discussed in chapter 1, "Numbers and Operations," older children should identify and explore number properties such as the commutative property (3 + 4 = 4 + 3), the associative property (7 + [3 + 5] = [7 + 3] + 5), and the distributive property + (8 × [5 + 9] = 8 × 5 + 8 × 9 = 112) and use them to compute with whole numbers.

Equation Race

This game gives children practice in creating equations using all four operations (+, −, ×, and ÷) and the aforementioned number properties. The object of the game is to see who can use five numbers along with any of the four operations to make a specified number.

Materials

You will need to make a set of cards (index cards work well for this) with the following 50 numbers: three cards for each of the numbers 1, 2, 3, 4, 5, 6, 7, 8, 9, and 10; two cards for each of the numbers 11, 12, 13, 14, and 15; and one card for each of the numbers 16, 17, 18, 19, 20, 21, 22, 23, 24, and 25. You should have two to six players for this game. Put the kids to work to make the deck. Check to see if the deck is complete when they have finished. Players will also need a pencil and paper on which to write their equations.

Procedure

Equation Race is played in rounds, with all the players playing at the same time. To start a round, mix up the 50 cards and place them face down. Each player chooses five cards and puts them face up in front of her or him. The player draws another card and turns it face up. That number becomes the goal value for that round.

The players then race using all five of their number cards and any of the four operations (addition, subtraction, multiplication, or division) to make an equation whose answer is the goal value. For example, if the goal value is 20 and a player drew 24, 3, 8, 2, and 4, the equation could be 24 + (3 × 4) − (8 × 2) = 20. Each number must be used only once, but they can be used in any order. The operations can be used as many times as needed. Warning: Not every combination of numbers can make a satisfactory equation, but students will get plenty of math practice finding this out.

The first player to write an equation equaling the goal value stands up and says, "Goal!" The player then has 30 seconds to show the equation that he or she created. The other players check the equation to see if it is correct. If it is, the equation-creating player gets one point. If it is not correct, the play continues. However, the player with the incorrect equation is disqualified. If no one can create an equation within a speci-fied time, the round is cancelled and no point is awarded. At the end of each round, reshuffle the cards and place them back down for the next round. Declare a winner when one player earns three points.

> Children in this age group should begin to represent the idea of a variable as an unknown quantity using a letter or a symbol—for example, $9 + n = 16$.

Riddle Me This

Children love riddles. Number riddles can help with mathematical thinking and be fun at the same time. In grades 3 to 5, multiplication and division are a large part of the computational curriculum. Children are expected to memorize all the "times tables," understand what is meant by multiplying and dividing, and be able to use math-ematical symbols to show that knowledge.

Materials
You will need paper, a pencil, and crayons or markers for this activity.

Procedure
Have your child visualize a picture of a multiplication problem—for example, five rows of squares with seven in each row would be a picture of 5×7. Then, have him or her write a riddle for this picture—for example, "5 of me makes 35. What am I?" Fold a piece of paper in half, with the fold going the short way of the paper, as shown. Write the riddle at the top of the paper near the fold. Next, have your child write the riddle using symbols just underneath the riddle—for example, "$5n = 35$." Lastly, your child should draw the picture he or she visualized on the *inside* of the folded paper and also write the answer to the riddle. This will allow your child to see the riddle and equation without giving away the answer. You can make more difficult riddles using larger num-bers—for example, "Nine of me makes 108," or "Five of me makes 75."

Your child should be encouraged to use let-ters for the missing number, a large dot between numbers to be multiplied instead of ×, and the solidus (/) for division in equations—for exam-ple, $^{56}/_8$ means 56 divided by 8.

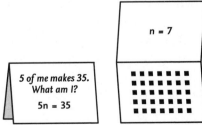

Unknown Concentration

As with other Concentration games, the object is to make a match between two cards. This time, however, the cards contain an equation with a letter used for the unknown and cards that tell what the unknown represents. For instance, a match would be made with one card that has "If $x = 7$, then $x + 9 =$ ___ ?" and a card with the answer "16."

Materials

Make a deck of 20 cards, 10 with equations and 10 with answers. You should have two or more players for this game. Some examples of equation types are:

Equation Cards	Answer Cards
If $p = 12$, then $p - 4 =$ ___	8
If $y = 5$, then $8y =$ ___	40
If $s = 8$, then $17 - s =$ ___	9

Procedure

Shuffle the cards and place them face down on the playing surface in four rows. Children take turns turning over two cards at a time to see if they can make a match. If the cards match, the player keeps them. If they do not, the player returns them face down on the playing surface. Play continues until all matches are made. The player with the most matches wins. You can make the game more difficult by increasing the difficulty of the equations.

> Children in grades 3 to 5 should be able to express mathematical relationships using equations.

Children of this age group should be able to take story problems and write the math sentence or equation that illustrates the problem. For instance: The fifth grade class was having an end-of-the-year cookout. There are 24 students in the class. Each will eat one hot dog. The hot dogs come eight to a package and the buns come six to a package. Hot dogs cost $1.59 per package and the buns are $0.79 per package. What is the cost of the food? Answer: $1.59 (24 ÷ 8) + $.79 (24 ÷ 6) = $7.93.

Story Problem Book

Materials
You will need plain paper, a pencil, sticky notes, assorted construction paper for making book covers, tagboard or lightweight cardboard, and a stapler or brads.

Procedure
This activity will cover several subjects at the same time: reading, writing, and math. Have your child choose a topic or hobby in which he or she has an interest, such as sports, music, books, or collectables. Then, your child is to write stories that include something about the chosen topic. Here is where the math comes in: instead of a traditional story ending, end the story with a mathematical question. For example:

Sue and her friend Ann love to listen to music. One day they talked Sue's mom into taking them to the mall so they could go to the music store. They looked at the CDs in the rock section and in the country section. The CDs were $16.95 each, including tax. If they each bought two CDs, what is the total cost? Answer: 2 ($16.95) + 2 ($16.95) = $67.80; or 2 ($16.95 × 2) = $67.80; or $16.95 + $16.95 + $16.95 + $16.95 = $67.80.

Your child can copy his or her story onto plain paper, illustrate it, and write the equation and answer on the bottom right-hand corner. To give the story a little intrigue, put a sticky note over the equation and answer. Write "Answer" on the sticky notes. This will cover the answer and allow the problem to be shared with others to see if they can get the answer. If sticky notes are not available, just glue a little flap of paper about the same size over the answer so that it can be raised to reveal the equation.

Your child can repeat this activity many times, and he or she can put similar stories together to make a book. Children will feel proud that they have written and "published" their own book.

> Upper elementary students should develop and use models to represent and explain mathematical relationships found in many different situations. They should use these models to draw conclusions about those situations.

Some of the models that students of this age group use are number lines, tables, charts and graphs (bar, pictograph, line, circle), diagrams or pictures, two-dimensional shapes or three-dimensional solids (cubes, cones, pyramids), geoboards, base-10 blocks to show models of whole numbers and decimals, and many other types of models.

Using these visual models allows students to see the situations more clearly so that they can draw conclusions.

Rectangular Array

To teach multiplication, division, perimeter, and area, schools today use a technique called **rectangular arrays**. These are visual models of what these concepts really are. A rectangular array is made using graph paper. For example, if you want a child to make a picture or model of the multiplication problem 5 × 9, you would draw a rectangle on the graph paper so that the rectangle had five squares for width and nine squares for length: a 5-by-9 rectangle. Students discover that if they count all the squares inside the rectangle, they have the answer to the multiplication problem. You can use the same rectangle to model division. If there are 45 squares in the rectangle and one side is nine squares long, then the other side must have five squares: 45 divided by 9 equals 5. You will find samples of the type of graph paper used for rectangular arrays in the Appendix of this book (see pages 205–208). However, any graph paper will do.

For third grade students, use ½-inch graph paper. Children at this level are expected to memorize their multiplication and division facts through the twelves.

Materials
Use graph paper of a suitable size for the age of your child, plain paper, scissors, glue, and a pencil or pen.

Procedure
Have your child make a rectangular array for each of the facts using the graph paper. Your child can cut this out and glue it onto a plain sheet of paper. Under his or her array, your child can write the related multiplication and division facts. For instance, if the rectangular array is 9 by 6, your child can write the following facts beneath it: 9 × 6 = 54, 6 × 9 = 54, 54 ÷ 9 = 6, 54 ÷ 6 = 9. Have your child make a new page for each family of facts. You and your child can put the pages together into a book that your child can use to aid in memorizing the facts. By using this method, your child not only will be memorizing the information, but will also have a good understanding of what multiplication and division mean.

Older students may need ¼-inch paper (see the Appendix, page 206), as they will make models using larger numbers. Fourth and fifth grade students will be multiplying and dividing using two- and three-digit numbers by two-digit numbers (for example, 52 × 16 = 832; or 832 ÷ 16 = 52). While it is impractical to have your child make a rectangular array for every multiplication and division problem, it is worth the effort to do a few in order for your child to be able to visualize just how big 52 × 16 really is.

See, for example, this rectangular array model for 52 × 16:

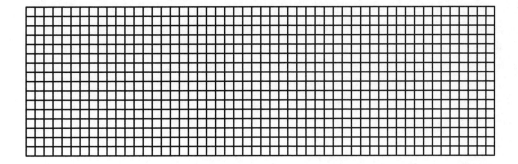

Children in upper elementary grades also should analyze change in various contexts. They investigate how a change in one unknown relates to a change in a second unknown. They also identify and describe situations with constant or varying rates of change and compare them.

An example of analyzing change might be investigating plant growth. Students plant seeds and then record how much the plant grows each day. The students could show this data in a table or on a graph. Since the plant, most likely, will grow at a varying rate, the children will be analyzing a change with rates that are not constant.

An example of change that is constant might be the distance someone covers while jogging at a set rate. Other types of constant rates of change might include increase or decrease, but at a set rate.

Weather Reporter

Materials
You will need an inexpensive thermometer, rain gauge, weather data from a newspaper, a television or access to the Internet, a 12-by-18-inch (30-by-45-cm) paper for a chart, and a pencil or pen.

Procedure
Working with weather data is exciting and mathematically challenging for children. Your child may wish to collect his or her own data using an inexpensive outdoor thermometer, a rain gauge, his or her own observations, or data from a newspaper or the Internet. Weather data is a prime example of varying rates of change. Your child will need to set up charts to record the data collected. The chart should include dates, cate-

gories for temperature and precipitation (other weather data collected from television news, newspapers, or the Internet, such as air pressure or wind data), and observations. Have your child analyze the change that he or she sees in each category. Your child can do this daily or weekly. If you live in a climate with cold winters, it is also a good way to explore negative numbers—10 degrees below zero or −10°F (−23°C). Your child can also use information gathered in the chart to make graphs. These show change in a dramatically visual way.

Literature Connection

One Grain of Rice: A Mathematical Folktale by Demi

Geometry

Geometry seems like a gigantic subject to be taught to little folks, particularly when we, as adults, remember the topic as a tangle of proofs and memorized theorems. Actually, geometry describes the world and universe all around us. Children are fascinated with the shapes they see everywhere they look. They make comparisons about how shapes are alike and how they are different. Those shapes are found in their homes, schools, playgrounds, and in nature.

Children are excited to learn that all those shapes can be measured and that all shapes, no matter how novel, take up space. As young people explore the world of shapes, they begin to describe what they discover. They learn that shapes have perimeter and area. They uncover that shapes can have shapes within them. The journey of exploring geometry in the elementary years takes them through finding shapes that are congruent or similar and the discovery of lines of symmetry. Their sense of spatial relationships is strengthened. With this exploration of shapes, children begin to see connections between counting, measurement, and other fields of mathematics. Their growing knowledge of geometry allows them to appreciate the beauty and construction of buildings and the environment around them.

As a parent, you can be an essential part of your child's exploration into the field of geometry. Take a moment to look at your own surroundings and you will be surprised at how much this particular field of mathematics permeates your everyday living. Through activities, games, and just taking the time to point out shapes you and your child see, you will strengthen your youngster's spatial sense and knowledge of the world of geometry.

Skills and Activities for Grades Pre-Kindergarten to 2

Children in the early years begin their study of geometry by sorting and classifying two-dimensional figures such as triangles and three-dimensional shapes such as cubes according to the characteristics they observe.

> By the end of second grade, children should recognize, name, build, draw, compare, and sort two-dimensional shapes (such as squares, triangles, and rectangles) and three-dimensional shapes (such as cubes, cones, and pyramids).

Although children begin to form concepts about shapes long before they enter school, in the early grades they spend considerable time refining those concepts. They must learn to recognize and name the shapes. Today's schools teach this through activities and play that has children build and draw the shapes. Then, teachers and parents can make comparisons to help students differentiate between them.

Wind Sock

Wind socks are a fun project to make with your youngster. You can use them to teach the three-dimensional shape called a cylinder. When making this project, use the words *cylinder, parallel, hollow,* and *circle* with your child. While it will seem like a fun art activity to your child, there are an abundance of geometric concepts to be learned—with a little direction from you.

Materials
You will need a 12-by-18-inch (30-by-45-cm) piece of construction paper or other stiff paper of similar size; markers, crayons, or paint; glue; crepe paper streamers or ribbons; a paper hole punch; string; and scissors.

Procedure
Using the paper, your child can create decorations of any kind with the markers, crayons, or paint. If it is near a holiday, encourage him or her to use the symbols associated with that day. Or, it may be fun for your child to be creative, drawing funny faces,

geometric designs, or animals. Then, have your child roll the sheet of paper into a cylinder. Keeping the ends parallel, help your child glue the paper 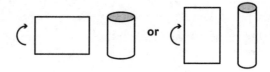  together to form the cylinder. Your child can roll the paper to make a 12-inch (30-cm) tall cylinder or an 18-inch (45-cm) tall cylinder. It will, of course, depend on the direction your child takes the picture.

Now, your child is ready to attach some streamers to the bottom of the cylinder. The number and the length are up to you both. To hang the wind sock, have your child punch a hole on either side of the top of the cylinder and attach a string.

Frozen Geometric Solids

It is sometimes difficult to find perfect examples of three-dimensional shapes, but here is an easy and inexpensive way to make your own.

Materials
The first things you will need are some containers. These need to be made of paper, capable of holding water, and of the correct shape for the solids you want to create. You can use milk cartons or juice cartons (the waxed paper kind in the pint or quart size) to make cubes and rectangular prisms. Frozen orange juice cans are great for creating cylinders. To make the cone, you may have to purchase cone-shaped paper drinking cups.

Procedure
You and your child can fill these containers with water, Kool-Aid, or gelatin and allow them to freeze or set overnight. The following day, remove the paper containers and explore the properties of the shapes. Have your child discuss how the solids are alike and different. Your child can eat the Kool-Aid and gelatin shapes when finished.

To make more permanent three-dimensional shapes, use plaster of Paris to fill the forms.

Literature Connection
Color Zoo by Lois Ehlert

> Primary school children should be able to describe characteristics and parts of two- and three-dimensional shapes.

In the beginning, children will use their own vocabulary to describe the shapes they see. They may describe a rectangle as looking like a door or say that the **vertex**, or corner, of a triangle is the "pointy part." You should not discourage this, since they are observing and describing characteristics; at the same time, you should try to introduce the correct terminology. Some characteristics that you may introduce at this age are the number of sides a shape has, the number of corners, whether the shape has straight or curved sides, and whether the shape is closed or has an opening, like the shapes of the letters *C* or *V*.

Stretch a Shape

This is a simple and entertaining way to teach the names and properties of the two-dimensional shapes.

Materials
All you will need is 2 yards (1.8 m) of 1-inch (2.5-cm) black elastic. (White elastic works just as well, but black doesn't show the dirt.) You need to sew the elastic together at the ends to form a circle, so you will also need a needle and thread. You should have three or four people participate, working cooperatively.

Procedure
Each person takes hold of the loop of elastic. One player names a shape, such as "square." The group, then, must form the elastic into a square shape and name as many properties as they can—for example, four sides, four corners, all sides the same length, sides are parallel, and so forth. If a game format is more interesting for the children, you can award points for the number of properties each player lists. The players should be able to make squares, rectangles, parallelograms, pentagons, hexagons, octagons (if four people are playing), triangles, trapezoids, rhombuses, and possibly circles and ovals.

Literature Connection
The Greedy Triangle by Marilyn Burns

> **Primary children should investigate and predict the results of putting together and taking apart two- and three-dimensional shapes.**

Through play and exploration, children discover that putting two shapes together sometimes results in a different shape. For instance, if you put two congruent right triangles together, you may have a square, a rectangle, or some other shape. Or, if you put two long, narrow rectangles together, you may have a larger and fatter rectangle. After they have practiced and explored putting shapes together, ask children what they think would happen if they put, for example, two squares together. Then, have them put the shapes together to see if their prediction was correct.

Children also take apart shapes. They can make predictions by asking questions such as, "What shapes would result if a square were split diagonally?" or, "What would the results be if the square were split in half horizontally?" They can then investigate to prove or disprove their predictions.

Would You Eat Out of This?

As with other fields of mathematics, young children need time to explore. This activity allows your child to create and make discoveries about shapes. The object is to make a container to hold a favorite snack. The snack is the reward for a functional design. The hardest part will probably be for you not to step in too soon. Your youngster needs time to explore using trial and error.

Materials
You will need sheets of 8½-by-11-inch (21-by-27-cm) paper to make the container. You will also need tape, a stapler, nontoxic glue, scissors, and crayons. The snack can be cereal, popcorn, small crackers, or animal crackers.

Procedure
Your child can create any type of container he or she wishes. It can be a cup, a basket made with a rectangular box and a handle, a boat shape, or whatever will hold the snack. Older children may see that they can make a cone. It is all right for your child to struggle a little bit. This strengthens his or her ability to problem solve and be creative. However, if you see too much frustration taking place, give a hint about where to start. Little hands may have a great idea, but may not have sufficient fine motor skills to create what they imagine. Let your child lead, but you can do the gluing or the stapling.

Once you and your child have made the container and decorated it, it is time to fill it with the snack. This is also a good time to discuss what shapes went into building the container.

You can use this activity several times, but each time encourage your child to make a new shape. Kids enjoy eating snacks from a container they have created on their own—and this is a great way to build a little self-esteem.

Literature Connection

Three Pigs, One Wolf, and Seven Magic Shapes by Grace Maccarone

> **Children in the primary grades should be able to describe, name, and interpret relative positions in space such as *under, above,* and *between*. Using a grid, like those found on a map, students in second grade should locate a position using simple coordinates such as "Go four right and six up."**

Students need to develop skills that relate to distance, direction, and positions that objects have in space. You can develop your child's knowledge of relative position by using stories that talk about where objects are located. Through stories that can be acted out, your child can see where the characters have moved. Also try demonstrating what is meant by *near* and *far,* or *over* and *under.* You and your child can make simple maps to represent objects in a child's room or other places in the home.

Bedroom Map

A map of your child's bedroom is an excellent start to understanding the much larger maps (city, state, and country) that he or she will encounter later in the school experience. It also lays the groundwork for coordinate geometry.

Materials
You will need a large sheet of paper, at least 12 by 18 inches (30 by 45 cm) in size, as the basis for the map. You will also need a pencil, scraps of colored paper, scissors, crayons or watercolor markers, and glue or paste.

Procedure
The difficult part for children of this age group is to visualize a floor plan from the aerial perspective. Have your child pretend he or she is a bird perched on the ceiling light looking down. What does the room look like from above?

Explore what the bed looks like. Is it a circle or a rectangle? What does the table or dresser look like from up there? Flat objects against the wall such as windows and mir-

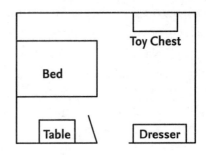

rors are difficult for children to imagine. Your child may need help realizing that flat objects only look like a line from the ceiling perspective. You can easily demonstrate this using a dollhouse.

Once you have discussed the aerial view, talk about the location of objects using *left, right, near, under,* and *over.* Discuss the geometric shape of the room. Is it a square or rectangle? Does it have parts cut out? (Some rooms have nooks and crannies.) Draw the shape on the large sheet of paper so that the outline fills most of the paper. Depending on the age of your child, you may need to assist in doing this. Have your child use the colored scraps of paper to cut geometric shapes to represent the bed, dresser, tables, toy box, wastebasket, rugs, and other objects found in the bedroom. Have your child place these cut-out shapes on top of the room outline to accurately show where the different pieces of furniture are located. When they are in the correct spots, your child can glue them in place.

When the map is complete, have your child tell about the location of the objects in the room. Encourage him or her to use those words that tell direction and relationships with other objects such as *under, above, left,* and *right.*

Literature Connection

Spaghetti and Meatballs for All by Marilyn Burns

> In the early grades, children should describe, name, interpret, and use the ideas of direction (left and right) and distance in moving through space.

Look Where You're Going

Even little tykes love to look at maps. This activity will introduce beginning map concepts and also be a tool to practice directions—left and right and north, south, east, and west.

Materials
You need only a map of your city or state and a Matchbox (small) car to do this activity.

Procedure

Unfold the map and let your child take several minutes to look at it. Your child will want to tell you what he or she sees and will likely have many questions. If your child does not discuss and discover the directional compass on the map, point it out and explain its function. You will need to help your child understand that north is toward the top of the map, south is toward the bottom, east is to the right, and west is to the left. (It may provide deeper understanding to position the map in accordance with true directions.)

Now, it is time to go for a drive. Let your youngster choose a road on the map (you may have to explain they are the lines that go from town to town). Have your child place the Matchbox car on the road and "drive" it according to directions, such as, "Go north on the road" or, "Go left or west on the road." City maps are great for going a particular distance because they are often on a block system—for example, "Go three blocks south and one block west. Turn right."

Another way to do this activity is to let your child drive the Matchbox car on top of any road on the map and tell you which direction he or she is going.

Literature Connection

Left or Right by Karl Rehm and Kay Koike

> Primary grade students should find and name locations with simple relationships such as "near to." Second grade students should begin to use coordinate systems such as simple maps.

Coordinate Pair Tic-Tac-Toe

Materials

For this game, you will need to make a grid on a large sheet of paper that is 12 by 18 inches (30 by 45 cm) or larger. The grid should have a 0 outside, but next to, the lower left-hand corner. You should letter the vertical lines "A" through "E" across the bottom and number the vertical lines up the side "1" through "5." You should have two players for this game.

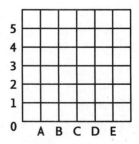

You will also need 12 small paper squares of one color for one player and 12 small paper squares of a different color for the other.

Procedure
Players take turns naming a coordinate pair. The first player says, for instance, "B3," and then places one of his or her small colored squares where Line B and Line 3 intersect. It is then the other player's turn. The first child to place four of his or her markers in a row—vertically, horizontally, or diagonally—wins. For young children, you should supervise the game to see that they are placing their markers accurately. It is permissible for players to try to block their opponent.

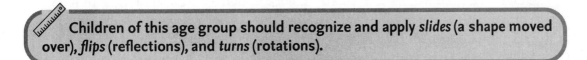

Children of this age group should recognize and apply *slides* **(a shape moved over),** *flips* **(reflections), and** *turns* **(rotations).**

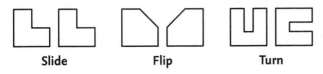

| Slide | Flip | Turn |

Children in the early grades begin to explore spatial relationships by noting what happens to shapes when they move. These motions or movement of shapes are called **transformations**.

Paper Quilt Blocks

Quilt blocks are both mathematical and an art form. When introduced to quilts, children learn many concepts related to geometry. Quilting is a study in shape, spatial relationships, and motions of shapes.

Materials
You will need examples of quilts (real or pictured), construction paper or assorted wallpaper samples, scissors, a quilt block pattern from the Appendix (see pages 212–213) or a quilt book, plain paper for quilt block backing, a pencil, lightweight cardboard for templates, and glue.

Procedure

To introduce a child to the world of quilts, spend time looking at patchwork quilts that are already made. Have your child explore the repeating patterns, name the shapes, and discover how shapes are flipped or turned. Your child can also examine color and material patterns. If you do not have access to quilts, look for quilt shows in your area. There are many books available that show pictures of quilts. Some catalogs sell quilts and would be a source for pictures.

The next step is to have your child make a quilt block out of paper. Stay with simple shapes such as squares and triangles for young children. The shapes should be congruent and cut from construction paper or other colored paper. An interesting variation to plain colored paper is wallpaper. Often, upon request, your local paint and wallpaper store may give you an old wallpaper sample book. This allows for many more choices.

You and your child will need to choose a block design. You can find these in many books, or there are some sample blocks in the Appendix. Have your child choose two or three types of paper for the block, depending upon the block that you choose. Cut out a supply of the squares and triangles from the colored or patterned paper, according to the directions for the block chosen. For young children, you may have to do the cutting; older children can make a template or pattern, trace around it on the back of the papers, and then cut the shapes out. Next, you or your child need to draw an outline of the block on a plain piece of paper. Blocks for children should be no smaller than 6 inches (15 cm) nor larger than 12 inches (30 cm).

Now, it is up to your child to assemble the small pieces onto the quilt block chosen. Your child will need time to manipulate the pieces, assembling and reassembling until he or she has achieved a pleasing arrangement. Once the arrangement is complete, have your child glue the pieces in place onto the quilt block outline. The younger the child, the more assistance he or she will need from you. But don't step in too quickly. This moving around of the pieces is where the learning takes place.

Literature Connection

The Quilt Story by Tony Johnston and Tomie dePaola

> **Children in grades 1 and 2 should recognize and create shapes that have symmetry.**

Figures have a **line of symmetry** if a mirror can be placed on that line and reflect exactly what the opposite side looks like. An example of symmetry would be the heart shape of valentines or a shamrock. These shapes have one line of symmetry because the sides only reflect one way, from left to right. Some shapes have more than one line of symmetry. A square has four. It can have a vertical line dividing it in half, a horizontal line, or two diagonal lines forming lines of symmetry.

**One Line
of Symmetry**

**Four Lines
of Symmetry**

Magic Picture Folds

Discovering symmetry can seem magical to the young mind. This project capitalizes on the unexpected appearing right before a child's eyes.

Materials
To do this activity, you will need paper and crayons.

Procedure
Fold a piece of paper in half—either way is all right. Open the paper and have your child color a picture next to the fold line. (Remember when, as a child, you made Valentine hearts by cutting out half of it on the fold.) Next, have your child go over the picture again, coloring heavily so that little of the white paper shows through. Refold the paper in half so that the colored picture is inside. Have the child rub the outside of the folded paper with the side of a pencil or with his or her fist. The paper needs to be rubbed hard enough to transfer the crayon colors to the other side of the paper, but not so hard that the paper is torn. When your child opens the paper, the picture "magically" appears. The fold on the paper is a line of symmetry causing one side to reflect the other. Children often want to repeat this activity several times to see if it really works each time. Each time your child does this, the concept of line symmetry is reinforced.

Variation: Mirror Symmetry
A variation of this project is to have the child draw and color half a picture on the fold (as was done in the previous example). Instead of refolding and rubbing, place a mirror next to the fold or line of symmetry and watch the other half of the picture appear.

Your child may want to check other pictures found in books or magazines to see if they have lines of symmetry. For instance, a picture of a person will have a line of symmetry if the child holds a mirror vertically on the center of the person—both sides of the face will appear as a normal face. However, if the mirror is centered horizontally across the person, the person will appear to have two heads or two lower torsos and not match what is on the backside of the mirror. Some pictures will have one line of symmetry, others may have more, and some may not have any. Your child will enjoy exploring this phenomenon.

> **Primary students should create mental images of geometric shapes using spatial memory and spatial visualization.**

Children develop spatial visualization skills by building or making designs and models using a variety of blocks, geometric shapes, or even real objects that have the standard geometric shapes. The key is for them to gain experience and practice manipulating shapes and objects. Spatial memory comes when they can "see" those shapes in their minds without having to build or manipulate the actual objects.

Take It Away

This simple game is based on building spatial memory.

Materials

You will need a group of small objects. The number of objects will vary depending on the age of your child. For very young children, you may want to start with five different objects. Second graders could probably handle 20 objects. You may need to experiment to find the appropriate number for your child. You should have two players for this game.

Procedure

Lay the objects out on a level surface. Give the first player a minute to look at them. Next, have that player turn so he or she cannot see the objects. The second player removes one object. When the object has been removed, the first player must turn around and try to name the missing object. Only one guess is allowed. If the first player names the missing object correctly, he or she earns a point. The second player now returns the object that was taken away to the playing surface. The objects can be rearranged. It is now the second player's turn to look away and then guess the object that was taken away. Play five rounds. The player with the most points wins.

To put more geometry into the game, use objects that have regular geometric shapes. Have the players name what was taken away and name the geometric shape.

Literature Connection

The Case of the Backyard Treasure by Joanne Rocklin

In the early grades, students should begin to recognize and represent shapes from different perspectives.

Children, through experience, begin to recognize that various forms of two-dimensional objects such as triangles and rectangles may "look" different from one another. They need to see a variety of these shapes to realize they are all still triangles or all rectangles. Triangles may look like right triangles or equilateral triangles. Rectangles may be long and skinny or almost square. With exposure, young children will begin to recognize that these shapes all belong to the same shape group. Likewise, children begin to look at three-dimensional shapes such as cubes and cylinders. When these objects are seen from a different angle, do they still look the same? Children will make these connections through exposure.

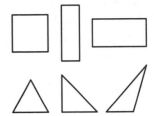

Feely Bag Perspective

You can use "feely bags" for many games and activities that require a child to simply feel an object or to make a random draw. They are easy to make.

Materials
You will need a plastic cup such as a 16-ounce plastic party cup or any plastic container with a large opening. You will also need an old sock (the longer the top the better), stiff cardboard, and scissors.

Procedure
To make a feely bag, slip the cup inside the sock. (The cup makes it easier for you to get your hand inside during this activity.) That's it—your feely bag is made!

For this activity, cut the basic two-dimensional shapes from stiff cardboard. You will want to make different types of triangles and rectangles and different sizes of squares, circles, and ovals. You may include pentagons, hexagons, and octagons. Younger children may only be able to tell you the number of sides, but not the names. That is all that is needed at this age. Put the shapes in the feely bag.

The object of the activity is for your child to put his or her hand in the feely bag, choose a shape, and describe as many properties of the shape as possible by feeling the shape. (By feeling the shape, then verifying it, your child develops visual memory.) If your child knows the name of the shape, he or she should tell it, too. Then, remove the shape from the feely bag and have your child see if it is like he or she visualized.

You can do this with three-dimensional shapes if you have them or can make them. You will need a larger bag if these shapes take up more space.

> Children of this age group should begin to relate ideas in geometry to ideas in number and measurement.

The exploration of geometry leads naturally to measurement and the use of numbers. As children build shapes, they automatically include "how long" or "how wide" in the description of those shapes. In the early grades, children may use nonstandard units of measurement. Children often use tiles (small, flat square pieces such as 1-inch [2.5-cm] ceramic tiles) to build two-dimensional shapes. Therefore, the measurement of a rectangle may be expressed as "nine tiles long and five tiles wide." The total number of tiles used to build the rectangle involves counting. These connections bring mathematics together as a whole.

Shapes and Estimating Measurement

Materials
You will need small manipulatives such as paper clips, dried beans, M&M's, and small cheese crackers as nonstandard units for measurement. You will also need standard measurement devices, such as a meter stick or yardstick.

Procedure
Children need to see geometry in their daily lives. As a regular activity, point out something in your home that has a geometric shape, such as a book (rectangle), plate (circle), or a potholder (square). Ask your child to name the shape.

Choose a group of small objects of uniform length for your child to use as a nonstandard measuring tool. Small children do not understand rulers and other more traditional measuring devices, but can measure using a series of small, same-sized objects (such as M&M's, paper clips, and so on). Have your child make an estimate as to how many of the small objects it would take to go around the outside edge of an everyday item. Then, let your child measure by placing the small objects all around the item. Discuss how close the estimation was to the actual measurement. Of course, this is the basis for the teaching of perimeter in the later grades.

Another activity you can do with common things found in your household is to have your child explore finding their area. The small measuring objects used this time must be square. How about small cheese crackers? Again, have your child estimate how many crackers it would take to cover the surface of the household item. Then, check the estimate by placing the small crackers over the surface while counting.

These two activities will help show your child that geometry is also integrated with measurement and counting. They are preliminary discoveries to later geometric concepts.

Literature Connection

Look Around! A Book About Shapes by Leonard Everett Fisher

> Children in the primary grades should recognize geometric shapes and structures in the environment and specify their location.

As children become aware of geometric shapes and their characteristics, they should be encouraged to locate them in buildings, in nature, and in the whole world around them.

Neighborhood Scavenger Hunt

Neighborhood Scavenger Hunt is similar to any scavenger hunt, but the objects to be found are geometric shapes.

Materials

You should have two or more players for this game. Make a list of two- and three-dimensional shapes for each player. The lists should have a space beside each item so that the player can write the name of a building or structure. Each person also needs a pencil.

Procedure

The object of this game is to look around the neighborhood and find a building, structure, sign, or other man-made object that contains one of the two- or three-dimensional shapes on the list. When players locate one of the shapes, they should write the name of the structure next to the shape on the list. The player who finds all the shapes wins. This is a great game for pairing up a young child with an older child. The older child can help supervise, write the object names, and also enjoy the hunt. If that is not possible, you can still have a scavenger hunt with just you and your child. The competition then changes from playing against an opponent to seeing if you can locate all the shapes on the list.

Literature Connection

Shapes in Nature by Judy Feldman
The Village of Round and Square Houses by Ann Grifalconi

Skills and Activities for Grades 3 to 5

Children in the upper elementary grades continue to analyze characteristics and properties of two- and three-dimensional geometric shapes, but they do so in a more precise manner than in the primary grades.

> Older students should identify, compare, and analyze the properties and characteristics of two- and three-dimensional shapes and develop specialized vocabulary to describe those properties.

Children of this age group begin to develop specific definitions for each of the different shapes, based on particular characteristics. For example, a rectangle is a four-sided shape with its opposite sides of equal length. The four corners are all right angles. Students have little difficulty understanding this definition when it applies to rectangles with two long sides and two shorter sides, but how about a square? Is it a rectangle? By definition it is, since it meets all of the characteristics for a rectangle. Older students discover similar relationships by careful comparison and analysis of shapes' properties.

Geometry Concentration

Materials

For this game, you will need to copy the set of geometry concentration game cards found in the Appendix (see pages 214–215). If possible, copy them onto cardstock or tagboard. You can also copy them onto paper, cut them apart, and paste them onto index cards. Your child should be able to help with this. The game can be played with one to three players. The players can use the Possible Properties List shown here and in the Appendix (see page 215). Each player also needs paper and a pencil.

Procedure

Place the cards face down on the playing surface in a rectangular pattern. The first player turns over two cards, deciding if the two cards are a match by naming a property both shapes share. You can find acceptable properties on the Possible Properties List. (Saying that objects share a *missing* property, such as "No right angles," is not allowed.) All players must agree that both cards have the property that was named. If correct, the first player keeps the two cards. If the first player names a property that is wrong or if the two cards do not share a common characteristic, the player returns the two cards, face down, on the playing surface. It is then the next player's turn. The game is over when no more cards match up or when all the cards have been played.

Variation

To make the game more difficult, have the players match up cards using two properties. (For example, both shapes have right angles and four sides.)

Possible Properties List

Number of sides	Right angle
Equal sides	Obtuse angle
Length of sides	Number of vertices
Parallel sides	Symmetrical
Perpendicular sides	Quadrilateral
Congruent shapes	Pentagon
Similar shapes	Hexagon
Acute angle	Octagon

Literature Connection

Sir Cumference and the First Round Table: A Math Adventure by Cindy Neuschwander

> Children in grades 3 to 5 should categorize two- and three-dimensional shapes according to their properties. From this, they should develop definitions for classes of shapes, such as triangles and pyramids.

As an example, triangles can be classified by the lengths of their three sides. Triangles with all sides the same length are called **equilateral triangles**; those with two sides the same length are **isosceles triangles**; and those with no sides the same length are called **scalene triangles**. Likewise, triangles can be categorized by the size of their angles. If one angle is square, it is called a **right triangle**; if one angle is larger than 90 degrees, it is an **obtuse triangle**; if all angles are less than 90 degrees, it is called an **acute triangle**.

Pyramids also can be classified by the number of sides, or **faces**. They may be examined for the shape found on each of those faces. A **square pyramid** has a square for its bottom or base and four triangles for its sides. A **triangular pyramid** has a triangle for its base and three triangles for sides.

How's Your Book Shaping Up?

Materials
You will need a pencil or pen, plain white paper, old magazines or catalogs, scissors, and glue. As an option, you can use a spiral notebook instead of the plain paper.

Procedure
Having your child put together a book is an enjoyable but challenging way for him or her to learn about the properties of specific two- and three-dimensional shapes. Have your child title each page of the book with the name of a shape. Your child may then write a list of properties that tell about that shape. Children in the third grade may need to copy definitions for their shapes, but by fifth grade, students can list the properties on their own. For example, to make a page about cubes, your child would write the following information at the top:

Cube
- A three-dimensional shape
- Has six faces
- Each face is a square

Your child should make a page with the appropriate title and properties for different shapes. Your child can make the pages on plain white paper that will be bound later, or he or she can use a spiral notebook.

After your child has put a heading on each paper, the fun part begins. Using old magazines or catalogs, have your child find and cut out pictures of objects, buildings, or everyday items that have those shapes. Then, have your child sort the objects according to the two- or three-dimensional shape it represents. Have your child glue the pictures onto the appropriate page of the book.

You may wish to do all the shapes listed here or only those that your child is currently studying for the grade level he or she is in.

LIST OF SHAPES

Two-dimensional	Three-dimensional
Circle	Cone
Hexagon	Cube
Parallelogram	Cylinder
Pentagon	Triangular Prism
Polygon	Square Prism
Quadrilateral	Rectangular Prism
Rectangle	Square Pyramid

Rhombus
Square
Trapezoid
Triangle

Triangular Pyramid
Sphere
Hemisphere

You can find definitions for these shapes in the Glossary.

Literature Connection

Shape Up! by David A. Adler

> Students in this age group should investigate, describe, and use reasoning skills about the results of *subdividing* shapes (dividing shapes into a combination of smaller shapes), *combining* shapes (putting shapes together to form a new shape), and transforming shapes (moving shapes by turning, flipping, or sliding).

Subdividing, combining, and transforming shapes are ways that children explore the relationships between shapes. If students are trying to determine the area of a shape, they may wish to subdivide them into sections and figure the area for each part. Take, for example, finding the area of a trapezoid. The shape can be subdivided into a square and two triangles. The area of the square can be figured, then the two triangles can be combined by transforming them into another square, with its area also figured. Then, the two areas can be added together.

Tangram Puzzles

A tangram is a set of seven geometric shapes that, when put together, form a large square. The seven shapes are two small triangles, one medium triangle, two large triangles, a square, and a parallelogram.

While at first glance tangram puzzles appear quite simple, they can offer some challenging problems that develop the geometric concepts of spatial reasoning, congruency, similarity, area, perimeter, and properties of polygons. Because of the puzzle nature of tangrams, they are also an excellent and enjoyable activity for teaching subdividing and combining shapes. In order to make the

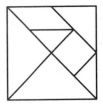

puzzles, you have to make flips, turns, and slides with the tangram pieces. Once your child has started playing with tangrams, he or she will have difficulty finding a place to quit. If your child likes puzzles, he or she will be hooked.

You can purchase inexpensive sets of brightly colored plastic tangram pieces from school supply catalogs. While not as colorful or long lasting, you can also make tangrams from paper. You can find a pattern for the pieces in the Appendix (see page 216). The next activity has directions for making tangrams from a square sheet of paper. This is also a good activity for teaching your child how to follow directions.

Making a Tangram Puzzle

Materials
To make the puzzle, you need one 8½-by-11-inch (21-by-27-cm) sheet of paper and a pair of scissors. For the second half of this activity, you will also need a copy of the following Tangram Shape Exploration Sheet.

Procedure
Fold the rectangular paper on the diagonal to form a square. Cut off and discard the excess paper. Unfold the square. Cut it in half on the diagonal.

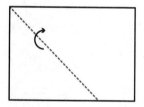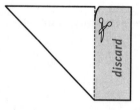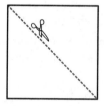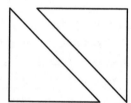

Take one triangle, fold it in half as shown, and cut along the fold.

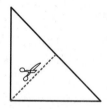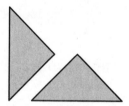

Take the other triangle and fold the top down to the base forming a trapezoid, as shown. Unfold and cut off the top.

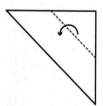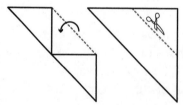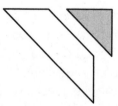

Cut the trapezoid in half along a center line. Fold one of the halves of the trapezoid to make a square and a triangle, and then cut. Fold the other trapezoid half to make a parallelogram and a triangle, and then cut.

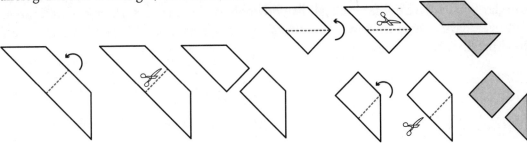

As with any new puzzle, your child needs time to explore. You may also want to allow playtime with the pieces. The following activity is an interesting way for your child to become familiar with all the pieces and see what can result when you combine pieces. Have your child utilize the following Tangram Shape Exploration Sheet below.

Ask your child if he or she can make these shapes with the tangram pieces—square, triangle, rectangle, trapezoid, parallelogram. Have your child record the number of pieces he or she used and draw a sketch of how he or she did it.

TANGRAM SHAPE EXPLORATION SHEET EXAMPLE

	1	2	3	4	5	6	7
Triangle			etc.				
Square			etc.				

Literature Connection

The Ancient Mystery of Tangrams (500 puzzles with a magnetic hardcover on which to work the puzzles)
Grandfather Tang's Story by Ann Tompert

Beginning in grade 3, children should explore similarity and congruence.

Similar figures have the same shape, but do not have the same size. **Congruent figures**, however, have exactly the same size and shape, regardless of their position. They can be flipped, turned, or slid.

Congruent Figures   **Similar Figures**

Comparing Congruent Shapes

Materials
For this activity, you will need two pieces of grid paper (1 centimeter size or larger; see the Appendix, pages 205–208), markers, and a pair of scissors.

Procedure
On one sheet of grid paper, have your child draw a shape—any shape will work, whether geometric or an irregular shape. Then, have your child draw the same shape sideways or upside down on the second piece of grid paper. The shapes should be congruent (the same size and same shape). To see if the shapes really are congruent, have your child cut out one of the shapes and place it on top of the other one. Your child can repeat this activity several times using a variety of different shapes.

If you have more than one child doing this activity, a matching activity can result. Put all the cut-out shapes in a pile and see if your child can match them with the ones on the grids.

Literature Connection
The Quiltmaker's Gift by Jeff Brumbeau

Older students should make predictions and test their conjectures about geometric properties and relationships. They need to justify their conclusions by developing logical arguments based on what they discovered when they tested their predictions and conjectures.

As children explore the world of shapes, they begin to form predictions and hypotheses about how one shape relates to another. For example, children may discover that several rectangles may have the same area, but as the dimensions of the sides get closer to one another, the perimeter gets smaller. (For example, rectangles of 3 × 4, 2 × 6, and 1 × 12 all have the same area: 12. The perimeters, though, change: they are 14, 16, and 24.) At this age level, children should be encouraged to make these "conjectures" and then test them out with models or drawings so they can justify their hypotheses. Then, children need to be able to communicate what they find out.

This is where you, as a parent, need to be available to listen to your child's theories, having your child tell you his or her reasoning and what he or she did to come to the conclusions reached. It is important that your child supports his or her thinking with reasons. True, these may not always be correct, but the process is the essential part. You can guide your child into more correct results by posing questions about his or her hypotheses.

Math Talk, Pure and Simple

Your child cannot necessarily practice this skill with a game or particular activity. However, there is much you can do to help your child make logical arguments for his or her discoveries about geometry. When you see your child building, drawing, or manipulating geometric shapes, take time to have him or her describe the activity. Ask questions about your child's models: "What two-dimensional shapes have you used?" "What would happen if you added a triangle to this part?" "Why do the perimeters get larger on rectangles with the same area but different dimensions?" You don't have to be a mathematical expert and know all the answers, but get involved in the exploration. It's all right to say, "I don't know. Let's see if we can figure it out."

Encourage the use of math vocabulary. Using the proper terms makes learning more precise and more detailed. Children greatly increase their learning of mathematics, and other subjects as well, when they have to tell directions, explain their thinking, give the steps, or just plain put into words what is going on in their minds. Being there as your child's audience will enhance his or her understanding many times over.

> Students in the upper grades should continue the study of location and movement that they began in the primary grades. They should begin using common language, but also develop more precise language using geometric vocabulary.

Children of this age group should be able to give directions, either verbally or in written form, for moving from one location to another—for example, "How do you get from your classroom to the gym?" or, "How do you get from your house to school?"

Geometric Pickup Sticks

This game is designed to strengthen your child's geometric vocabulary. The terms used are *parallel lines, perpendicular lines, line segments,* and *intersecting lines.* You can find the definitions for these words in the Glossary. They are concepts needed in giving location directions.

Materials
For this activity, you will need 12 toothpicks. You should have two players for this game.

Procedure
The first player releases the bundle of 12 toothpicks onto a flat surface. He or she then identifies toothpicks that form parallel lines, perpendicular lines, line segments, and intersecting lines. One point is earned for each correctly identified item. Then, it is the second player's turn to drop the toothpicks and proceed in the same way as the first player. The game is played for five rounds. The player with the most points wins.

> **In grades 3 to 5, students should make and use *coordinate systems* (map grids using numbers or letters along the bottom and the side) to specify locations and to describe paths.**

This age group is taught to use coordinated pairs of numbers—for example, (2, 6)—to locate a specific place, or **point**, on a grid map. The first number refers to the numbers across the bottom of the map, and the second number refers to the numbers along the side of the grid. All grids begin in the lower left-hand corner. This corner is 0. The notation "(2, 6)" tells you to go over two lines to the right and go six lines up on the grid.

Describe paths to show movement on the map. For example: Ted was delivering pizza. He left the pizza shop, went three blocks north and one block west to Bill's house. Then, he delivered an order to Sue's house by going four blocks south and two blocks east. Upon

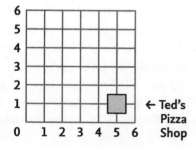

leaving Sue's, he went two blocks north and one block east. What are the coordinates where Ted made his last delivery?

Connect-the-Dots Secret Picture

This is an activity based on the old connect-the-dot puzzles you may have done as a child. The difference with this activity is that your child must create his or her own picture using a piece of grid paper and ordered pairs (a number and a letter).

Materials
All that you will need is paper, a pencil, some 1-centimeter grid paper (½ inch grid paper will work, too), and a ruler. See the Appendix, pages 205 and 207, for grid paper that you can photocopy.

Procedure
To get started, here is a practice activity. These directions for a Secret Picture give practice using ordered pairs. First, you must make a coordinate system or grid using ½-inch or 1-centimeter grid paper. Outline a large square having at least 12 squares on a side. Put a 0 outside the lower left-hand corner. Label the lines across the bottom with the numbers 1 through 12. Label the lines going up the left side with the letters of the alphabet, A through O. Be sure to put these labels outside the square.

Have your child try to make the following picture by placing a dot on the intersection of each number and the letter on the grid below. Then, have your child use a ruler to connect the dots. The Secret Picture will appear.

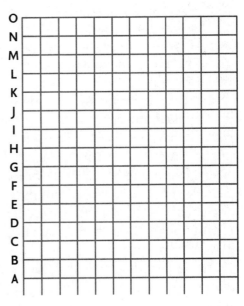

1. (5, A)	8. (8, N)
2. (11, A)	9. (7, M)
3. (11, B)	10. (8, K)
4. (9, B)	11. (7, K)
5. (9, K)	12. (7, B)
6. (8, K)	13. (5, B)
7. (9, M)	14. (5, A)

To create original Secret Pictures, use the following directions.

Have your child sketch out a simple picture outline on the plain paper. Using the grid paper, you should label the **x-axis** with numbers (numbers should label the lines going vertically). Then, label the **y-axis** with letters (letters should label the lines going horizontally). Your child is now ready to transfer his or her sketch onto the grid paper. The outline may need to be adjusted to take advantage of the lines on the grid paper.

Now comes the creative part. Using the pairs of numbers and letters, have your child write directions for someone else to make his or her picture.

Mystery Guess and Check

Teaching coordinate pairs is not always easy, but this game for two players makes it fun and offers the repeated practice that is so essential.

Materials

You will need several sheets of 1-centimeter grid paper (see the Appendix, page 205), two index cards, two pencils, a ruler, and markers. You should have two players for this game. You will need to put a barrier between the two players so that they cannot see each other's game board; a large book will do.

Procedure

The game board for this game is a coordinate system or grid. Make the grids (one for each player) on the 1-centimeter paper. Outline a large 15-by-15 square on the grid paper using the ruler and markers. Starting at the lower left-hand corner (outside the grid), label it "0." Now, label each vertical line across the bottom of the square with the numbers "1" through "14." Do the same with the horizontal lines going up the left side of the square. Each player will need to make a playing piece from the index card. The piece is a right triangle, with the two sides next to the right angle each being 7 centimeters long. The children are now ready to play.

The object of this game is for a child to discover the three corners of his or her opponent's hidden triangle. To begin, each player "hides" the triangle anywhere on his or her grid. The triangle should be placed so that each corner touches a point where two lines intersect, or cross, on the grid.

The first player guesses an ordered pair such as (8, 3). Remember, the first number denotes the number across the bottom, to the right of 0, and the second number is the column that goes up, along the left edge. The opponent then answers, "Corner check" (if any corner of the triangle touches the named point), "Side check" (if any of the three sides of the triangle touches the point named), "Inside check" (if the point is inside the triangle), or, "Out of bounds" (if the point is outside the triangle and no part of the triangle touches the point). Players must keep track of the information they receive in order to finally discover the exact location of the hidden triangle. It is then the second player's turn.

The player who correctly locates the three corners of his or her opponent's triangle wins.

Literature Connection

Plotting Points and Position (Math for Fun) by Andrew King

> Students in the upper elementary grades should try to find the distance between points along horizontal and vertical lines of a coordinate system (a map grid).

Students are taught to figure distance on a map grid by subtracting the coordinate pairs of numbers. For instance, if the two points are both on a horizontal line and the points coordinates are (2, 6) and (2, 1), the difference is found between the unlike numbers (6 − 1 = 5). Therefore, the distance between the two points is five. The same is done to figure distance on the vertical lines. If the two points are (7, 8) and (4, 8), the distance between the two points would be three (7 − 4 = 3).

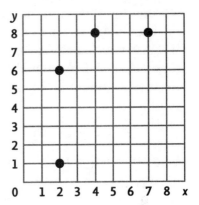

Neighborhood Map

Drawing a map is an exceptional first step in being an efficient map reader. By having to create a map, your child has to understand all the elements that go into making a map a communication tool. It also allows him or her to understand that maps are symbolic, but also represent real objects in the world.

Materials

All you will need is plain paper, grid paper (see the Appendix, pages 205–208), and a pencil. However, if you want color, you may also use markers or crayons.

Procedure

Take a walk around your neighborhood with your child. Talk about the things that you see, discussing the types of buildings, what geometric shapes you see, and the number of blocks between different locations. You may want to take some paper or a notebook to jot down notes, distances, lists, and so on.

When you return home, you should set up a coordinate system like those described in previous activities. The numbers of the horizontal and vertical grid lines need to be related to the largest number of blocks that your child wants to show on his or her map.

Next, your child should make a map key to relate which symbols will be used on the map to show where certain buildings and places are located. An example would be that a small box represents houses, a triangle represents a church, or a rectangle with a small flag represents a school. Your child is now ready to put the symbols on the map, locating them so that they are the correct number of blocks from one another and the correct direction (north, south, east, or west) in relation to one another.

Now, have your child give the ordered pair for each symbol. For instance, the school is at (3, 9) and your house is at (3, 2). What is the distance between the two? Your child can find the answer by subtracting the 2 from the 9, resulting in a distance of seven blocks. If the places are not on the same horizontal or vertical grid line (both were on 3), where simple subtraction is done, the distance can be figured as ___ blocks east and ___ blocks north. Your child can then add the two numbers to figure the distance. (This distance assumes that you follow the street grid and do not "fly" directly from point to point.)

Variation

A variation of this activity would be to have your child make a map of an imaginary village, locating all the necessary types of buildings a town would need. Your child can use the same procedure for finding distances between locations. As an extension, have your child build the village. LEGOS, Tinker Toys, Dacto Blocks or any other building materials will work. Even using juice cartons, small boxes, and other assorted household "junk" will work. This is super for the creative side of learning.

Literature Connection

The Fly on the Ceiling: A Math Myth by Julie Glass
Look Both Ways: City Math by Time-Life Books

> Children in the upper elementary grades should continue to study transformations. They should predict and describe the results of sliding, flipping, and turning two-dimensional shapes.

While younger children need to actually slide, flip, or turn shapes in order to describe transformations, students in the upper grades should be able to predict the position of a shape when given a description of the transformations or movements done. They also should be able to describe what movements occurred when shown a shape in a beginning position and then in an ending position.

Map Transformation

This game for two players provides practice identifying flips and turns. As an added bonus, it also gives practice learning the names of states or provinces.

Materials

Both players need a map of the United States with the state names printed on them (or a map of the country in which you live). You can find an outline map of the United States in the Appendix (see page 217). You should have two or more players for this game. Each player will also need a supply of thin paper suitable for tracing and a pencil.

Procedure

Each player should write "Top" at the top of his or her page. Then, each player should trace the outline of one of the states on the same paper. Out of sight of his or her opponents, each player will decide to make a second tracing in which the state has been flipped or turned. To make a flip, a player would need to flip the first drawing of the state over and then retrace it onto another sheet of paper. The players are now ready to start the game. The first player shows his or her state to the opponent. The opponent must name the state and tell if it is flipped, turned, or as it appears on the map. If the second player gives correct responses, then he or she gets one point for correctly naming the state and one point for identifying the transformation. If neither answer is correct, the first player wins a point. Players take turns. The winner is the player with the most points after five rounds. In the case of a tie, one more round is played to break the tie.

> **Older students should be able to describe a motion or a series of motions (such as turning a half turn or flipping horizontally and then turning a quarter turn) to show that two shapes are congruent.**

Students in the lower grades prove that shapes are congruent by physically manipulating the shapes, laying one shape on top of the other. In the upper grades, students should be able to visualize the outcome without having to physically move the pieces and to be able to give precise directions as to what would need to be done to prove they are congruent—for example, "Rotate the shape a quarter turn and flip it horizontally."

Pentomino Puzzles

A pentomino is figure that is made up of five congruent squares. The squares must be joined so that at least one side is touching another square's side.

A pentomino also can be flipped to show a mirror image.

Your child can make 12 pentominoes using the definition above. Using 1-inch grid paper (see the Appendix, page 208), have your child explore making all 12. Some pentominoes can be folded to form cubes. Have your child cut out the pentominoes and experiment folding and taping to see which ones will form cubes and which will not.

Another activity that involves using congruent pentominoes and moving them by flipping, sliding, and turning is using one pentomino shape to tessellate (or tile) an area.

Materials

You will need paper at least 9 by 12 inches (22.5 by 30 cm) or larger, 1-inch grid paper (see the Appendix, page 208), a pencil, and crayons or markers.

Procedure

Think of this activity as if you were tiling your kitchen floor. Choose one pentomino to use as a pattern for tiling. Your child is to use the one pattern, tracing it over and over to cover the paper as if covering the paper with tiles. There can be no gaps. Your child can flip, turn, and slide the pentomino. When all the tiles are in place, your child can color the pentominoes in a pattern.

This activity requires a child to visualize moving geometric shapes, but it also allows the shapes to be manipulated using the one pentomino as a template.

> Students should identify and describe line symmetry and rotational symmetry in two- and three-dimensional shapes and designs.

A shape has line symmetry if it can be folded in half so that its two parts exactly match.

The fold line is called a line of symmetry. Figures can have more than one line of symmetry, as shown by this diagram:

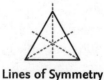

Lines of Symmetry

Alphabet Symmetry

Materials
All you will need for this activity is paper, a pencil, and markers.

Procedure
The object of this activity is to discover lines of symmetry found in the alphabet. Have your child print the upper case, or capital, letters approximately 1 inch (2.5 cm) high on the paper. Then, have your child trace over this with marker. This will allow your child to erase without destroying the alphabet. Using the pencil, your child is to discover how many lines of symmetry each letter has. Your child can also categorize the letters as having lines that are horizontal, vertical, both horizontal and vertical, or diagonal. (Answers: The horizontal letters are B, C, D, E, H, I, K, O, and X; the vertical letters are A, H, I, M, O, T, U, V, W, X, and Y; the letters that are both horizontal and vertical are H, I, O, and X; and the letters that are diagonal are O and X.)

Pinwheel

A shape has **rotational symmetry** if you can turn it less than one full rotation around a central point and the shape or figure looks the same as it did before the rotation.

A perfect example of rotational geometry is the pinwheel. It can be

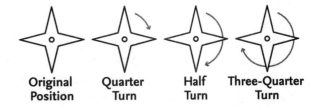

| Original Position | Quarter Turn | Half Turn | Three-Quarter Turn |

turned a quarter, half, or three-quarters of a turn and still looks like it did when in its original position. Here are directions for making a pinwheel.

Materials
To construct the pinwheel, you will need construction paper, scissors, a ruler, straight pins, and a thin wooden dowel. (You can use plastic straws in a pinch.)

Procedure
Have your child cut a 6-by-6-inch (15-by-15-cm) square from construction paper. He or she should draw two diagonal lines so that the square is divided into four triangular parts. Then, have your child cut each diagonal 3 inches (7.5 cm) toward the center of the square, but no farther. Your child should have four connected triangular sections. Have your child fold the right-hand corner of each triangular section to the middle so that the points slightly overlap, and then put a straight pin through all the layers of

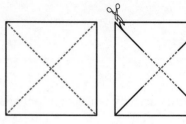

paper in the center. Your child can then stick the pin into the wooden dowel and test the pinwheel to make sure it turns freely. Your child now has a visual model of rotational symmetry. Discuss how the pinwheel looks the same after it has been rotated only one quarter of a turn. Do the same with half and three-quarter turns. Now, go have fun. It's time for your child to take the pinwheel outside and watch it race in the wind.

Literature Connection

Sam Johnson and the Blue Ribbon Quilt by Lisa Campbell Ernst

> **In order to solve problems, older children should build and draw geometric objects so that they can see relationships between shapes.**

Upper elementary students should use visualization, spatial reasoning, and geometric modeling to solve problems.

There is a Chinese proverb that says: I hear and I forget; I see and I remember; I do and I understand. This is particularly true when children are trying to see geometric relationships. The more children build, draw, make, and experience, the more they will understand. Maybe if we had had this approach to geometry when we were in school, those proofs and theorems would not have seemed so monstrous to some of us.

Marshmallow and Toothpick Geometry

Materials
All you will need is a large bag of miniature marshmallows and a box of toothpicks.

Procedure
Have your child use the marshmallows and toothpicks to construct two- and three-dimensional shapes. Your child can use these materials like Tinker Toys.

Ask your child to make:

A square	A cube
A rectangle	A pyramid with a square base

A triangle　　　　　A pyramid with a triangular base
A parallelogram　　A rectangular prism
A pentagon　　　　A triangular prism
A hexagon

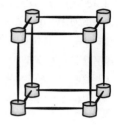

Your child can count and measure sides. He or she can measure and identify angles as right, obtuse, or acute. Your child can relate the faces of three-dimensional figures to a two-dimensional shape. He or she can count vertices and edges.

Have your child construct his or her own fantastic shape and discover the two- and three-dimensional shapes that were used.

If your child likes LEGOS and Tinker Toys, this activity will be a hit.

Literature Connection

Building Toothpick Bridges by Jeanne Pollard

> **Students in grades 3 to 5 should create and describe mental images of objects, patterns, and paths.**

Older elementary students should be able to mentally *see* objects and their movements without having to always build or manipulate. For instance, children should be able to solve the following problem without actually moving the paper:

If there is a triangle in the lower left-hand corner of a piece of paper and the paper is turned a half turn clockwise, where will the triangle be then?

How Did You Do?

One objective of the NCTM standards is to have children be able to think about and communicate mathematical ideas. Children should be able to do this both verbally and in written form. This activity gives practice communicating about shapes in written form and causes children to rely on mental images in order to complete the shapes.

Materials

You should have two players for this game. You will need a set of tangrams (see the Appendix, page 216) for each of the two players. Each player will also need paper and a pencil.

Procedure

The two players sit back-to-back or have a barrier between them. Each player makes a design using the tangram pieces. They do not need to use all seven pieces, but must use at least four. Each player sketches the design on one paper. Using a different paper, each player writes the directions or recipe for making the design. The recipe should use mathematical vocabulary and be clearly written so that the other player could draw the design without seeing it. Each player keeps the original sketch as a check for the recipe. When both players have finished their recipes, they will trade them. Have the children see if they can build or draw their partner's design using only the recipe the partner gave them. When both children have completed their designs, have the two players compare their designs with their partner's original sketch. How did they do? Did they follow the recipe carefully? Were the directions clear? Could they be improved?

Literature Connection

Janice VanCleave's Geometry for Every Kid: Easy Activities That Make Learning Geometry Fun by Janice VanCleave

> **Children of this age group should be able to identify and build a three-dimensional object from two-dimensional representations of that object.**

Two-dimensional representations of a solid figure are called **nets**. They are actually like patterns drawn on a piece of paper that could be cut out and folded to make a three-dimensional figure. This is an example of a net for a cube.

Children in the upper grades should be able to look at just the pattern, or net, and be able to tell what three-dimensional figure could be made.

Thinking in Three Dimensions

Solid figures are shapes that take up space. They are often, though not always, made of plane shapes called polygons. A polygon is a two-dimensional shape with straight lines (squares, rectangles, hexagons, triangles, and so on). A net of a solid figure shows those faces and how they connect as if the solid figure were laid out flat. Your child will need practice visualizing a two-dimensional form as a three-dimensional one.

Materials

In the Appendix (pages 218–220), you will find several nets for various three-dimensional solid figures. You will need to copy these to use. You will also need scissors and tape.

Procedure

At first, have your child cut out the nets and assemble them into a solid shape, using tape to hold them together. Next, simply show your child the nets and see if he or she can tell which solids they represent.

> **Upper elementary students should be able to identify and draw a two-dimensional representation of a three-dimensional object.**

This is the reverse of the last skill. Students in grades 3 to 5 should be able to look at a three-dimensional solid figure and draw the net or pattern using grid paper.

Designing Geometric Solids

Materials

You will need scratch paper, a pencil, 1-inch grid paper (see the Appendix, page 208), a ruler, scissors, and glue or tape.

Procedure

After studying the net or pattern for the cube shown previously, have your child try to design nets for the other three-dimensional shapes, such as rectangular prisms or pyramids with a square or triangular base. To start the process, have your child count the number of faces and discover the two-dimensional shape of each face. On scratch paper, have your child draw each face. At this point, your child may be able to see how the pieces could be joined together so that, if they were folded, a three-dimensional shape would be made. If this seems too difficult, have your child cut out each face and move the pieces around until he or she finds a possible answer. (There is more than one way to create a shape.)

Once your child has discovered a solution, he or she is ready to carefully draw the solution on 1-inch grid paper, using a ruler to get a straight line. You or your child will need to add flaps to some of the sides if your child wishes to cut out the net and fold it into the three-dimensional shape. The flaps are used to glue the shape together.

> Students should use geometric models to solve problems in other areas of mathematics.

As already illustrated in the previous chapters, geometric models such as number lines (negative numbers), rectangular arrays, shapes, and blocks for patterning are used to solve problems. Geometric models are closely related to solving measurement problems.

The best way for kids to understand math of any kind is to use it in real life. Geometry and measurement go hand in hand with many arts and crafts projects. Whether it is building birdhouses or making crafts, the hands-on experience increases learning tenfold compared to just reading how to measure or work with geometric shapes from books. Besides learning new skills, children's self-esteem is raised when they can take pride in having actually made something for themselves. Here is a quilt project that, with a little guidance, fourth and fifth grade students can do.

Quilt Block Pillow

Quilt projects are a perfect example of the integration of geometry and measurement. Quilts are by nature a study in shape. They are also a real-life practice in careful and accurate measurement. Here are directions for making a simple quilt block using the Roman Square pattern (see the Appendix, page 213). You and your child can then finish the block into a 12-inch (30-cm) throw pillow.

Materials

Roman Square pattern (see the Appendix)
Pencil
Lightweight cardboard for template
Scissors
¼ yard (22.5 cm) light-colored
    cotton fabric
¼ yard (22.5 cm) dark-colored
    cotton fabric
Pins
All-purpose thread (1 spool should
    be plenty)
Sewing needle
Ruler, marked to ¼ inch (0.6 cm)
Tape measure

Thin quilt batting, 13 × 13 inches
    (33 × 33 cm)
½ yard (45 cm) cotton fabric for the back
    of the pillow
Safety pins
Darning needle
Embroidery floss (2 skeins in a color that
    goes with the fabric)
1½ yards (1.4 m) pre-ruffled eyelet
    (optional)
Polyester stuffing or 12-inch (30-cm)
    pillow form
Sewing machine (optional)

Procedure

Instruct your child to do the following. Your child should be able to do both the measuring and the sewing with a little guidance from you.

To Make the Quilt Block

1. Copy the block pattern from the Appendix onto lightweight cardboard. Cut out the cardboard to make a template.
2. Decide if you want the squares to have the light fabric or the dark in the center of each square. Using a pencil, trace around the template on the wrong side of the fabric. You will need to make eight of the rectangles on one color and four rectangles on the other.
3. Cut out all the rectangles.
4. Pin a rectangle from each color together along the longest edge, right sides together.
5. Measure in from the pinned edge ¼ inch on both ends. Draw a line connecting both marks. This is the sewing line. (Adults do not usually need this drawn sewing line, but children do in order to have even seams.)
6. Sew the two pieces together on the sewing line using a small running stitch. Use a knotted double thread for strength.
7. Sew the third rectangle to one of the two pieces that were just joined. Use the same procedure—measuring ¼ inch (0.6 cm), drawing a sewing line, and sewing—to complete one square. You have just completed one-fourth of the block.
8. Repeat the procedure three more times. Be sure to keep the same pattern for all four squares—light, dark, light or dark, light, dark.
9. When all four squares are completed, it is time to join them together to finish the block. Do this by turning one square perpendicular (ah, a geometry word) to the other. Pin the two blocks with right sides together, mark the ¼-inch (0.6-cm) sewing line, and sew.
10. Do the same with the other two squares.
11. Now, join the two halves of the block by pinning the right sides together. Be sure that the halves are turned so that each square in the block is perpendicular to the one next to it. Check to see that the centers on the two halves are matched. Mark the ¼-inch (0.6-cm) sewing line and sew. Hurray! The block is finished.

To Complete the Pillow Top

1. Cut two square pieces from the fabric—one for the backing, slightly larger than the quilt block, and one the same size as the quilt block for the back of the pillow.
2. Cut one square piece from the batting, also slightly larger than the block.
3. Now, make a sandwich: Roman Square quilt block, thin batting, and then the slightly larger square cut from the backing material.
4. Use safety pins to pin the sandwich together, placing one pin in the center and one in each square of the block.

5. Thread the darning needle with a long piece of the embroidery floss. Use a double strand, but do not knot it.

6. Starting in the center, sew down through all the layers in the block, pulling the floss through but leaving 3 inches (7.6 cm) on the top side. Then, come up through all the layers approximately ⅛ inch (0.3 cm) from where you started. Cut off the floss so that it is the same length as the strands you left on top. Using a square knot, tie the strands, then tie a third time. Cut the tails to ¾ to 1 inch (1.9 to 2.5 cm).

7. Continue placing ties over the block, 4 inches (10 cm) apart. Work from the center out.

Applying a Ruffled Edge (optional)

1. Measure and figure the perimeter of the finished block. Cut the pre-ruffled eyelet 3 inches (7.5 cm) longer than the perimeter.

2. Pin the eyelet around the edge of the quilt block so that the ruffle is lying toward the inside of the block. It should be pinned so that the sewing line will be ¼ inch (0.6 cm) from the edge of the block sides.

3. Sew the eyelet in place around all four sides of the block using a small running stitch. Where the two raw edges meet, fold the cut ends over so that the raw edges are hidden. Sew in place.

Finishing the Pillow

1. Pin the second square cut from the backing fabric on top of the pillow block, right sides together.

2. Using the running stitch of the ruffle as a guide (or ¼ inch [0.6 cm]), sew the backing in place on all three sides. This step is best done on a sewing machine to add strength to the pillow. On the fourth side, leave an opening large enough to insert polyester stuffing or pillow form.

3. Turn the pillow cover inside out, stuff, and using a needle and thread, close the opening.

Literature Connection

Sweet Clara and the Freedom Quilt by Deborah Hopkinson

Older students should begin to recognize geometric ideas and relationships as they apply to other subject areas and to problems found in the classroom or in everyday life.

Dream Bedroom

What kid hasn't dreamed of redecorating his or her bedroom with everything he or she has ever wanted! This activity allows that dream to be explored and at the same time results in many educational experiences. Your child will discover that geometry has real importance in his or her everyday life. Measurement will be linked as part of the exploration. This also becomes a good lesson in real-life economics.

Materials
You will need paper, a pencil, a yardstick or measuring tape, ½- or ¼-inch grid paper (see the Appendix, pages 206–207), old catalogs featuring home and decorating items, and an old catalog order form.

Procedure
The beginning of this project is for your child to sketch, then measure the perimeter of the bedroom. Your child will need to understand inches, feet, and yards. He or she can record the measurements on the sketch. Your child should measure doors, windows, and closets, since he or she will be making a floor plan of this room. In a separate list, your child may want to measure the perimeters of the major pieces of furniture that will remain in the dream bedroom.

The next step is to draw the floor plan using the grid paper. Fifth grade students should be encouraged to draw the plan to a scale. Third graders may need to estimate the placement of objects in the room.

Now, for the dream part! Using the catalogs, your child can locate the new furniture, computers, televisions, stereo, drapes, bedspreads, and more that would be his or her ideal. If your child wants new carpet or flooring, then he or she should figure the area. Your child should list all the new materials or objects on paper along with the dimensions, page number, and price. After your child has selected objects for the new room, have him or her see if they will fit in the floor plan.

When your child has narrowed the list to what will reasonably fit in the bedroom, he or she is ready to fill out the catalog form. This is a real-life activity. When your child has written all the information on the form, have him or her total the cost. This figure will probably be a shock.

Most kids do not realize how expensive things needed for everyday existence can be. Maybe they will now see why they cannot have everything that they want. This is a beginning step or activity toward being responsible money managers.

While this activity is time consuming, it shows how math skills are really integrated in life outside of school. Your child may not even recognize that he or she is doing math. Sometimes a child's perception is that math is only something that is done in school out of a book. It is great when your child can see the application side of his or her studies.

Literature Connection

A Cloak for the Dreamer by Aileen Friedman

Measurement

Measurement is the most widely used area of mathematics. It permeates our everyday existence. How our lives would change if we did not measure time! Could we get through the day? We measure distance and length during our drive to work and in many of the tasks we do both on the job and at home. We monitor weight through daily activities such as buying produce at the market, mailing a package, or the ever-present quest to lose a few pounds. How often do you check the weather to find out the predicted temperature for the following day so that you can make or alter plans? Do you cook? If so, you use the measurements for volume and capacity with each recipe. Hobbies, arts and crafts, sports—the list goes on and on for the many ways that our lives are affected by measurement. You probably take measurement for granted and never stop to think of its importance in your life. It's just there.

Skills and Activities for Grades Pre-Kindergarten to 2

In the early grades, children should recognize the characteristics of length, volume, weight, area, and time.

Young children begin to learn about the different properties and characteristics of the various measurement units by looking at, touching, and comparing objects. They decide which stack has more by looking at them and seeing which is larger. They decide which object is heavier by lifting two objects and feeling the difference. To see which toy truck is longer, young children line them up and compare. Adults help with this process of recognizing measurement characteristics each time they say, "That is a large book" or, "That ribbon is too short."

As a parent, you should also initiate the concept of time in activities that are related to your child. Simply pointing out the time on the clock in relation to what your child is doing is the first step—for example, "Look, it is twelve o' clock. It's time to eat lunch." When reading bedtime stories, a discussion of the time of year, season, or month that is in the story will help your child develop time concepts. Finding the sequence (what happened first, next, and last) of that same story is good for teaching both measurement concepts and reading comprehension.

These are all examples of children learning through exposure—through the physical manipulation of objects and the comparison of those objects. Most important is the mathematical language and vocabulary that parents and, later, teachers provide in conjunction with that exposure.

Exploring Nonstandard Units

Materials
Choose a nonstandard unit of measurement for your child to use. Some possible choices might be toothpicks, envelopes, the child's hand or foot, Popsicle sticks, or pencils. You will also need paper and a pencil.

Procedure
With your child, choose several objects around your home to measure (for example, the objects' length, height, or width). You and your child will need to write the names of the objects in a list. Have your child measure each object using the nonstandard measuring unit you have chosen. You or your child can record the measurements next to the list of objects you made—for example, "Sofa = 10 envelopes long." A good follow-up activity is to discuss the results of the measurements by comparing which is the longest (or shortest, and so on). Your child can also order all the measured objects—for example, from shortest to longest. He or she may need help putting them in order by just looking at the number. If your child measured small objects, you may wish to physically move the objects into the correct order, which helps your child realize that the measurement numbers correlate to the relative size.

In the early grades, children should measure using several of the same-sized object, such as beans or paper clips laid end to end.

Primary children might not be ready for traditional measurement tools. A kindergartener or first grader's first tool for measuring is using multiple objects that are all alike, laid end to end and counted.

Gummy Worm Measurement

Materials
You will need the book *Inch by Inch* by Leo Lionni. It is a classic book that most children's libraries will have. You can also purchase it from most major bookstores. Use gummy worms for a nonstandard measuring unit. You will also need 10 objects to measure, paper, crayons, and a pencil.

Procedure
Read *Inch by Inch*. Discuss how the worm measured the birds. See what your child thinks about the nightingale's request to measure her song. Can you measure a song by the inch? Can you think of a different way to measure a song? Have your child choose 10 objects to measure, using the gummy worms as a nonstandard unit. For each object, have your child lay gummy worms end to end to measure the length. Your child may also draw and color a picture of the object. Have your child record the number of gummy worms needed for each measurement. Of course, when the measuring is done, eating gummy worms is a good reward for a job well done!

Towering Blocks

Linear measurement includes length, width, distance, and height. Many activities focus on length or width. Here is one that concentrates on height. Children need to be aware that measurement goes up.

Materials
You will need some type of block that can be stacked—wooden cubes, Dacto, or LEGO blocks will work. You will also need a pencil and paper for recording the number of blocks used.

Make a recording sheet with these headings across the top:

Picture	Estimate	Measurement

Procedure

Your child will choose an object with height to measure and draw a picture of the object on the recording sheet under the "Picture" heading. Then, he or she will estimate how many blocks tall the object is and write it down under "Estimate." Have your child make a tower of blocks next to the object and then count the number of blocks in the tower. This is the actual measurement. Have your child record this under "Measurement." Your child should compare the estimate to the measurement. Repeat the procedure for other objects.

To make this into a game, two or more players could each make an estimate and record on individual recording sheets. The two players can take turns building the block towers. The player whose estimate is closest to the actual measurement gets a point. Play five rounds. The winner is the player with the most points.

Literature Connection

The Biggest Fish by Sheila Keenan
Ten Beads Tall by Pam Adams

> By the end of second grade, students should be able to use a single measurement unit repeatedly to measure something larger than the unit. For instance, students learn to use a single yardstick to measure a room.

As adults, the skill of using a yardstick or meter stick and moving it to measure large objects or areas seems easy and obvious. However, it denotes a big jump in understanding for youngsters. It often requires a partner—one person to mark where the end of the measuring stick is and another to move the stick forward. There is also the problem of counting and keeping track of how many moves were made. Next, what do you do if you get to the end of the object or area and you cannot fit in another whole measuring stick? For second graders, it is probably best to round off the measurement to the nearest yard or meter. You can introduce the concept of mixing yards and feet, but primary students are not expected to use conversions from one measurement unit to another.

String Measurements

This activity not only helps children compare lengths, but also teaches an important measurement skill: lining up the measuring tool with the end of the object measured.

Materials

Cut several pieces of string, varying in length from 2 inches (5 cm) to 18 inches (45 cm). You will also need paper, crayons, and tape.

Procedure

Demonstrate for your child how to line up the end of a string with the end of an object to be measured. Your child should then choose a string and try to find an object in your house that has the same length. When your child has located the object, have him or her draw and color a picture of the object on the paper and tape the string to the drawing. After your child has finished with one string, you may want to check to see if he or she is correctly aligning the string with the end of the measured object and locating something about the same length as the string. Have your child try again with the other lengths of string.

Literature Connection

Long, Short, High, Low, Thin, Wide by James Fey
Inch by Inch by Leo Lionni

> Primary students should compare objects and order them from least to greatest (or the reverse) using the characteristics associated with length, volume, weight, area, and time.

During these early years, children begin to see relationships between objects, such as the fact that an orange is larger than a lemon. They then extend this to comparing more than two objects. Now, they may notice that a melon is larger than the other two and put them in order: lemon < orange < melon. Likewise, children will do the same with ordering objects according to length—for example, "I'm taller than my sister, but mommy is taller than me." They make similar discoveries with weight, area, and time. You, as a parent, can encourage this exploration in relationships by asking appropriate questions, such as, "Which is smaller, heavier, or longest?" or, "Can you put these in order?"

Is It Longer, Shorter, or Just the Same?

As an introduction to using a ruler and comparing lengths, this activity provides more exploration of measurement concepts.

Materials

Collect a variety of household objects or toys of different lengths (both less than and greater than 12 inches [30 cm]). You will also need yarn or string, three index cards or small pieces of paper, a pencil, a ruler, crayons, and a large sheet of paper.

Make two large, overlapping circles on the floor using string or yarn to make a Venn diagram. You should label the three sections of the overlapping circles "Shorter," "Same," and "Longer." Simply write one word (*Shorter, Same,* or *Longer*) on each of three individual index cards or small pieces of paper and place them in one of the three sections, making sure to put "Same" in the center. **Venn diagrams** are used routinely in elementary schools to help students sort information and see the relationships among the groups that have been sorted.

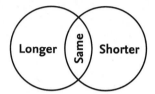

Procedure

Your child will "measure" each object using the ruler and determine whether the object is longer, shorter, or the same length as the ruler. He or she will then place each object in the correct section of the overlapping circles, or Venn diagram. When your child has measured and sorted all the objects, he or she may draw a picture of the Venn diagram built on the floor that includes the measured items. Some children may need help drawing the overlapping circles.

Your child can repeat this activity using other measurement tools, such as a yardstick or meter stick, tape measure, or a 6-inch (15-cm) seamstress gauge.

Literature Connection

Is It Larger? Is It Smaller? by Tana Hoban
Lulu's Lemonade by Barbara deRubertis

> Children at the primary level should begin measurement using nonstandard units and proceed into using standard units.

The use of standard units of measure, such as inches, pounds, or quarts, is a very abstract idea for young learners. Therefore, our adult measuring tools of rulers, bathroom scales, and measuring cups have little meaning for young minds. These children are still in the concrete stage, where they must have objects to see, touch, and move. For this reason, schools today teach primary students to measure using nonstandard units such as paper clips, beans, macaroni, and so forth. For example, if a first grader were to measure a pencil, he or she would lay paper clips from end to end along the side of the pencil and count, finally concluding, "The pencil is six paper clips long." The child easily sees this, incorporates counting units of measurement, and sets the stage for understanding standard units of measurement. Measurement for weight is taught using a balance scale. A child puts an object to be measured on one side of the scale and then uses objects of the same weight, such as marbles or pennies, to make the scale balance. The child then counts the marbles—another demonstration to set the stage for measuring in pounds or grams.

By the end of second grade, children will gradually move into using standard units of measure. They will measure length to the nearest inch or centimeter. Their balance scales will use weights that are marked in grams. They will read time to the nearest half hour. This transition should not be too difficult if children have a good foundation in using nonstandard units of measure.

Discovering the Inch

This is a delightful activity that combines literature and math, introducing children to standard measurement units.

Materials
Once again, you will need the book *Inch by Inch*. You will also need cardboard or heavy paper to make an inch ruler, scissors, a standard inch ruler, pencils, and crayons.

Procedure
Reread the book *Inch by Inch* to your child. It is a story about an inchworm that measures birds. Using the cardboard, help your child make a ruler that is marked off only in inches. Use the standard ruler to accurately place the inch marks on the ruler.

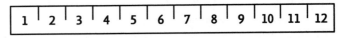

Your child can then decorate the ruler across the bottom with inchworms. Now, your youngster is ready to explore measurement with a standardized unit. Have him or her measure objects in your house to the nearest inch. Do not worry about half inches. If an object is halfway or more between two inch markings, call it the next inch up; if it is halfway below, call it the lower inch. Using a ruler with only inches makes measurement tools much more understandable to small learners.

Families by the Yard

Here's an activity that involves the whole family.

Materials

You will need a large ball of string, scissors, and a yardstick or meter stick.

Procedure

You and your child will measure the height of each family member by cutting lengths of string that are the same as their height. Then, use the yard or meter stick to figure the actual heights. Do not figure to the exact yard, foot, and inch; measure to the nearest yard and half yard—for example, "Daddy is 2 yards tall, Mommy is over 1½ yards tall, and my sister is 1 yard tall."

Literature Connection

How Tall Are You? by Joanne Nelson
Inch by Inch by Leo Lionni

Pre-kindergarten to grade 2 students should learn to select the correct unit of measurement for the object being measured and choose the appropriate tool to do so.

As children progress from the use of nonstandard units to using standard units of measure in second grade, they should appropriately use inches and centimeters for length and be able to differentiate between the two rulers. They should be able to tell time to the half hour and interpret the meaning of the numerals and days of the week on a calendar. Second graders should know that weight is measured in pounds and grams and choose scales to measure that. They should understand that measurements of capacity are measured using cups, pints, and quarts, though making conversions from one unit to another is still too abstract for this age group.

Guess What Tool to Use

As children near the end of their primary school years, they should have had many experiences measuring various quantities, both in school and at home. Second graders should be able to select an appropriate measuring instrument for a specific quantity.

How about turning practice into a road game? To help fill those sometimes tedious driving times, play the following guessing game.

Materials

No materials are needed.

Procedure

Think of a specific object, such as a car or a bunch of grapes. (Examples don't have to be something you see out of the window.) Ask a question, such as, "I want to know how long a car is. What tool should I use?" Your child should respond with an appropriate measurement tool, such as a ruler or yardstick. To initiate this game, you may want to give your child two choices, one correct and one incorrect—in this case, a ruler or a bathroom scale. As he or she becomes more proficient, drop the choices and let your child decide what to choose.

Literature Connection

How Big Is a Foot? by Rolf Myller
The Inch Boy by Junko Morimoto

Steps to Measuring with a Single Measurement Tool

In order to master the concept of using a single measurement tool to measure something larger than the tool, children need repeated experiences. For first grade students, have children practice using nonstandard units such as an envelope or a pencil to measure the length of a table. The smaller measuring tool is easier for little hands to manipulate. Then, you may wish to graduate to using a 12-inch (30.5-cm) ruler. You can informally introduce the standardized unit for the foot. By the end of second grade, children should be able to handle using yardsticks or meter sticks to measure rooms in the house, the length of the backyard, or the size of the garden. The important skill to be stressed at this level is placing the beginning of the measurement tool after moving it forward to exactly where the tool originally ended.

Children will also need to count the number of moves made to find the measurement. If keeping track of the number of moves is a problem, have your child make a tally mark on a piece of paper each time he or she moves the measuring instrument. Your child can then count the tallies when the measuring is complete.

Literature Connection

Twelve Snails to One Lizard by Susan Hightower

Primary age children should use many tools to measure, including rulers (inches and centimeters), balance scales, yard and meter sticks, clocks, and calendars.

This is where teachers yell, "Help!" There simply is not enough time in the school day or year for kids to get all the practice and help that is necessary for mastering the measurement tools. Have calendars in your home? How about one for your child's bedroom? You and your child can write special events on the calendar, and your child can count the days until that event happens. Ask your child to tell you the time using household clocks. First graders tell time to the nearest hour; second graders tell time to the nearest half hour. You may even wish to buy a wristwatch for your youngster. Please, please, please buy an analog watch (one with hands)! Digital watches are fine for older children who have already mastered telling time, but younger ones learn little from a digital timepiece. If you are measuring anything, include your child—whether it is making a shirt, building a doghouse, or weighing the fruit at the supermarket. It's that constant, everyday practice that will make all the difference in your child's success with measurement concepts.

The discussions so far have explored linear measurement. Children also need practice in measuring weight, capacity, time, and temperature. You can introduce these all as incidental learning when they come up in your daily lives. However, the following are activities for more direct instruction.

Comparing Weights

Materials
You will need scales for this activity. Balance scales, which can be purchased for less than $20 from school supply catalogs, are the most concrete and easiest way for primary students to understand weight. However, a standard kitchen scale also works well.

Procedure
Have your child choose two objects to weigh. Holding both objects, he or she estimates which is heavier. The child can record or tell the estimate to someone else. Then, the child can weigh the objects on either type of scale to confirm the estimate.

Using a kitchen scale, your child can also practice the concept of weight by choosing two small household objects, estimating which weighs more, and then weighing both objects to confirm the estimate.

What Time Is It?

How many times have you been plagued with questions such as, "How long before we go?" or, "When will Johnny be over?" In this activity, you may find a solution to the repeated questions, and you may also help teach your child to tell time.

Materials
You will need paper, a pencil or pen, a clock, and a timer.

Procedure
Draw a simple clock face on a piece of paper that shows the time the special event will happen. Your child can compare the drawing to a real clock, knowing it is time when the two clocks match.

Another easy way to work in a little practice is to set a timer to go off on the hour or half hour, and then ask your child to tell you the time.

Literature Connection
All in a Day by Mitsumasa Anno
Big Time Bears by Stephen Krensky
How Little, How Much: A Book About Scales by Franklyn Branley

> **Primary level children should develop a sense for common measures in order to make comparisons and estimates.**

Young children should be encouraged to estimate how long or heavy something is or how much time has passed. After they have made the estimate, your children can make actual measurements using either nonstandard or standard measurements. With practice, children's estimates will get closer and closer to the exact measure and move into the realm of a true estimate, not just a wild guess. This ability to estimate and compare is many times more valuable in our day-to-day living than exact figures. For example, it may not be that critical that you buy exactly 1.48 pounds of ground beef—about a pound and a half will do.

Estimation and Capacity

As you have noticed, many activities in this chapter include estimation first, followed by actual measurement. This repetitive practice of estimating helps develop the common sense about measurement we need as adults. When you measure, it is important to know if your answer is reasonable, and so being good at estimating lets us make that determination.

Kids love this activity. A little warning, though: it can be messy.

Materials
You will need several pounds of a fine, dry substance to use for measuring. Rice is ideal, but small beans or sand will also work. You will also need a large container such as a plastic dishpan to hold the rice or sand; a plastic drop cloth or a sheet; a variety of wide-mouthed containers having different shapes and sizes; measuring cups; masking tape; and a dark crayon.

Procedure
Place the dishpan filled with rice or sand in the center of the drop cloth. First, your child will make an estimate of the number of cups a chosen container will hold. Next, your child will use the measuring cups full of rice or sand to fill the container. Your child should count the number of cups it takes to actually fill the container. Using a small piece of masking tape stuck on the container, the child can use the crayon to write the number of cups it holds. Your child should then follow these steps for the rest of the containers. Then, he or she can order the containers from least to greatest, in terms of their capacity.

The drop cloth makes cleanup easy, since it can be lifted with any spilled rice in it and poured back into the tub.

You can do this same activity using water—a bit of a mess at the sink. Instead, using all plastic wide-mouthed containers, you can try it in the bathtub. Turn bath time play into a learning experience!

How Long Does It Take?

Materials
You will not need any materials for this activity.

Procedure
Have your child guess or estimate the amount of time it takes to complete everyday activities. Examples might be:

How long does it take to drive to Grandma's house?
How much time does it take to walk to school?
How long does it take to clean my room?
How many minutes does it take to take a bath?

After he or she has made an estimate, help your child figure the real time it takes for each activity and compare it to the estimate.

Literature Connection

The Fattest, Tallest, Biggest Snowman Ever by Bettina Ling
Just a Minute by Teddy Slater

Skills and Activities for Grades 3 to 5

> Upper grade students should not only recognize but also fully understand the properties of length, area, weight, volume, and the size of an angle. They should be able to choose the appropriate type of unit needed to measure each of those properties.

By the time children reach grades 3 to 5, they also feel comfortable in their understanding of when and what to measure with the unit of measure that applies to each situation.

At this level, children begin to measure area and the sizes of angles. Children are first exposed to "square corners," or right angles having 90 degrees. From this, children explore other angles using the right angle as a comparison for size—for example, "Is the angle larger (or smaller) than a right angle?" This will tell them that the angle must have more than (or less than) 90 degrees.

Size up a Tree

Exploring the various measurements of a tree provides a child with practice using different skills and may even offer a surprise to adults. Do you know how to measure the height of a tree from the ground?

Materials
You will need a yardstick or meter stick, string, paper, a pencil, a ruler, and, of course, a good-sized tree.

Procedure
To measure the trunk, begin by measuring 4½ feet (1.4 m) up from the ground on the trunk. Place a string around the trunk at this height. You and your child can measure the length of the string using first the yardstick and then the meter stick and then record both answers. Your child has found the tree's circumference.

To measure the crown, have your child choose five of the tree's longest branches. On the ground, your child should place a marker under the tip of the longest branch out of the five. Have him or her locate a long branch on the opposite side and place a marker beneath its tip on the ground. Have your child measure between the two markers on the ground, using both measurement tools, and record the measurements. Your child has found the spread of the tree's crown.

To measure the height, you will need to stand at the base of the tree. Your child will back away from the tree, holding the ruler vertically in front of him or herself. Keeping his or her arm straight and locked, your child should stop walking when the ruler and the tree appear to be the same height. Your child may need to close one eye to line it up. Standing in the same spot, have your child rotate the ruler horizontally, so it looks level with the ground, and then move the ruler sideways, so that one end is on the base of the tree. Be sure your child keeps his or her arm straight and locked and the ruler level. You should walk to the spot that appears to your child as the opposite end of the ruler, walking parallel to the ruler. Have your child measure how many feet you walked. Your child has just figured the tree's height.

Literature Connection

Measuring Penny by Loreen Leedy

At this age level, children should understand the need to measure using standard units and become familiar with both *English* (measurement units commonly used in the United States) and *metric* systems (measurement units used around the rest of the world).

As children move from using nonstandard units, such as the length of their feet, to standard units, such as the 12 inches that equal 1 foot, certain realizations occur. They will discover that if Johnny measures the length of the room with his feet and states that the room is 15 feet long, Sara, using the same method, may measure and find it to be 18 feet. The problem, of course, is that the units of measure are not standardized. Another problem with nonstandard measures are that gaps can result from using multiple objects. Take, for instance, measuring the perimeter of a book using beans. It is difficult to get the beans to touch perfectly without any overlap. Also, individual beans are not uniform in size.

As students move into measuring area and volume, the problems with nonstandard measurement increase. Can you truly figure the area of a rectangle by covering the area with beans? Or, what nonstandard unit would you use to find the volume of the shoebox? None of these would be accurate measures.

By the end of fifth grade, students should have a good understanding of the basic measurement units for both English and metric systems. Not only should they have memorized the names of the units, but upper elementary students should also have basic mental images of what those measurements represent—for example, a paper clip weighs about a gram, their math book weighs about a kilogram, or a yard is approximately the distance from their fingertip to their nose.

Students of this age group should be familiar with the following units of measure:

English units: inch, foot, yard, mile, ounce, pound, cup, pint, quart, gallon, Fahrenheit.
Metric units: centimeter, decimeter, meter, kilometer, gram, kilogram, milliliter, liter, Celsius.

Family Metric Smile

Metric measurement is of the same importance as our English measurement. In school, both systems are taught and used equally. Even in the United States, the metric system is routinely used in most scientific disciplines and many sporting events. Your child probably already feels much more comfortable with metrics than you do, having already worked with the system in the first and second grades.

The following activity is an interesting project that involves the whole family in metric measurement.

Materials
You will need a metric measurement tool marked off in centimeters. There are several common tools that would work. Cloth or plastic tape measures today have both inches and centimeters on them. You can purchase these for about one dollar anywhere sewing supplies are sold. Many rulers and yardsticks also contain both systems. You will also need paper, a pencil, and crayons or markers.

Procedure
Your child will measure the smile of each member of the family in centimeters and record the length of each person's smile. Next, your child will order the measurements from least to greatest. Who is the person in the family with the biggest smile?

Your child can also find the total length of all the smiles. Do the family smiles equal a meter? How many decimeters long does your family smile?

As an option, have your child draw and color a smile the same length as the total. This can be the "Family Smile."

Ruler of the House

This game involves many measurement skills—including the use of English units, metric units, and the estimation of length.

Materials
You will need small pieces of paper or index cards, paper, pencils, and English and metric measurement tools (such as rulers, measuring sticks, or tape measures). You should have two or more players for this game.

Procedure
Have your child make a set of 12 to 15 measurement cards. Write one measurement on each card or slip of paper using a variety of English and metric measures, such as 2 feet, 25 inches, 3 yards, 30 centimeters, 2 meters, and so on. Shuffle the cards or slips of paper. Have each player draw one card. Then, have the players choose an object in the room (or house) that they think has the same measurement as the card. The players then each write down the name of the object they predicted to have that measurement. The players each measure the object they named and record its measurement. The player having an object's actual measurement closest to the measurement on the card he or she drew earns a point. The winner is the player with the most points after five rounds.

Literature Connection

How Tall, How Short, How Far Away by David A. Adler
Super Sand Castle Saturday by Stuart J. Murphy

> In grades 3 to 5, students should be able to make simple conversions in measurements, such as inches to feet or yards; centimeters to meters; cups to pints, quarts, or gallons; milliliters to liters; ounces to pounds; or grams to kilograms.

This is where the fun begins! Here is another area of mathematics that requires plain, old-fashioned memorization. In the English system used in the United States, there is very little pattern for children to draw upon: 12 inches in 1 foot, 3 feet in 1 yard, 36 inches in 1 yard, 5,280 feet in 1 mile; 2 cups in 1 pint, 2 pints in 1 quart, 4 quarts in 1 gallon; 16 ounces in 1 pound, 2,000 pounds in 1 ton. This is quite a quagmire, and children often flounder as they try to retain all the facts and do the computations needed in order to make conversions.

The metric system, while still requiring some memorization of the different unit names and their order, has a definite pattern. It is all based on 10, like our number system. There are 10 millimeters in 1 centimeter, 10 centimeters in 1 decimeter, 10 decimeters in 1 meter, 100 centimeters in 1 meter, and 1,000 meters in 1 kilometer; 1,000 grams in 1 kilogram; and 1,000 milliliters in 1 liter. See the pattern? Once children learn the unit names, it is a much more user-friendly system of measurement. Children can easily make conversions, since all the units are multiples of 10. Do you suppose this could be why the rest of the world uses the metric system?

Milliliter vs. Liter

You are probably familiar with the 2-liter soda bottle, but have you stopped to look at the labels of other containers holding various liquids found in your house? Many are marked with an L (liter) or mL (milliliter). An eyedropper holds 1 milliliter of liquid, and 1 liter is equal to 1,000 mL (or, of course, ½ of a 2-liter bottle). Show and explain these two metric measures of capacity to your child.

Materials
You will need five household products labeled with mL or L, tape, paper, and a pencil.

Procedure

To give your child some familiarity with these two metric measures of capacity, take a food or liquid product from your shelves and cover the label with a small piece of paper and tape. You may find the label written in both English and metric measurements. Have your child estimate the number of milliliters (mL), or liters (L) if using a larger container. Do this with five products. Your child can then arrange the products from least to greatest. Remove the label covers to see how closely the estimates and order match the actual capacities.

As a side activity, have your youngster add the milliliters to see if all the products would make a liter. If the totaled products are more than a liter, are they closer to 1 or 2 liters? If there are two children doing this activity, change it into a game format by having each child write his or her individual estimates and record the order of the products on paper. The person closest to the actual measurement for each product earns a point, and the most correct order of products also earns a point.

You can also do this activity using ounces and pounds.

Measurement and Me

You know how anxious kids are to find out how tall they are. Why not measure the entire body? It is great practice!

Materials

You need very little for this activity—just paper, a pencil, and a cloth or plastic tape measure.

Procedure

On the piece of paper, your child will draw a picture of him or herself standing and facing forward. He or she should leave space around the picture to record estimated and actual measurements of various body parts. Once the picture is complete, your child will estimate the length, width, or circumference of a particular part of the body, such as the waist. He or she will write the estimate next to the waist in the picture and label it "Est." Next, have your child measure his or her waist in either inches or to the nearest half inch or centimeter. Have your child record that below the "Est." and label it "Actual." Have your child continue estimating and measuring other parts of his or her body.

Here is a list of parts to measure:

Around the head	Length of leg
Around the neck	Length of foot
Around the chest	Length of thumb
Around the waist	Length of big toe

Around the hips   Width of foot
Around the calf   Width of hand
Length of ear   Width of ear
Length of arm   Overall height

For practice making conversions, have your child take the larger measurements, such as the chest, waist, or leg length, and change the inches to feet and inches or change centimeters to decimeters. Your child can convert his or her height into yards and feet or meter and decimeters.

MEASURING ME

E [**Estimate of measurement**
A [**Actual measurement**

Around the head: E: _____ A: _____

Around the neck: E: _____ A: _____

Length of arm: E: _____ A: _____

Around the waist:
E: _____ A: _____

Around the hips: E: _____ A: _____

Length of leg: E: _____ A: _____

Overall height: E: _____ A: _____

Width of ear: E: _____ A: _____
Length of ear: E: _____ A: _____

Around the chest: E: _____ A: _____

Width of hand: E: _____ A: _____

Length of thumb: E: _____ A: _____

Around the calf: E: _____ A: _____

Length of foot: E: _____ A: _____
Length of big toe: E: _____ A: _____

Students of this age group should discover the idea that measurements in the real world are often not exact, due in part to the imprecision of measurement tools that are used and in part to human error.

Children should be made aware that measurements vary according to how carefully the measurement tool is aligned with the object and how carefully the person doing the measuring reads the instrument. Also, most measurement tools used in our day-to-day existence are not that precisely made. Two people can measure the same object and come up with slightly different readings. In a sense, measurement is a finely tuned estimation when used in the real world.

Just Prove It!

Nothing teaches like a demonstration.

Materials
You will need paper, pencils or pens, and two yardsticks, meter sticks, or rulers.

Procedure
Have your child and someone else (you or another child) each measure the length of the living room or family room. Use two different measuring instruments marked off in the same units. Each person records his or her measurement to the nearest half inch or centimeter. Are they the same? If there is a difference, could it be the measuring tools?

Try it again, but have each person use the same tool. Are they still different? Could it be human error? The larger the quantity measured, the more chance there is for error.

You can do this same type of activity with other measuring tools. Try it with scales, measures for liquids, clocks, or thermometers.

Literature Connection
The Librarian Who Measured the Earth by Kathryn Lasky

In the upper grades, children should explore what happens to measurements of two-dimensional figures, such as its perimeter and area, when the figure is changed in some way.

Sometimes one measured property, such as area, will remain the same, while another, such as the perimeter, changes. For instance, suppose you had several shapes with the area of five squares. The following figures all have the same area of five squares. Are their perimeters the same? No, they vary from 10 to 12 units.

Likewise, if the perimeter is kept constant, does the area change? Break five strands of uncooked spaghetti into two equal parts (10 pieces total). Build various polygons (many-sided shapes made of three or more straight sides) using all 10 pieces and figure the area. Are the areas all the same?

These kinds of explorations cause kids to stretch their mathematical thinking and reasoning. If approached as a quest or puzzle, they can be entertaining as well.

Changing Perimeters and Areas

Materials
You will need several sheets of centimeter grid paper (½-inch grid paper will also work; see the Appendix, pages 205 and 207), a pencil, scissors, and string.

Procedure
Have your child trace around his or her hand on the grid paper. He or she can figure the area by counting the squares inside the outline. Remember to have your child piece parts of squares together to make whole squares (for example, two halves, three-quarters of a square, and one-quarter of a square). Have your child record the area of the hand on the grid paper.

Have your child figure the perimeter of his or her hand by laying a string around the outline, cutting it, and measuring its length with a ruler. Have him or her record the perimeter on the grid paper also.

The objective now is for your child to use the string to find something else in the house that has the same perimeter. When your child has located an object, have him or her place it on another sheet of grid paper, trace around it, and figure its area by counting squares. Are the two perimeters the same?

Another time, you may want to try this activity by having your child trace around his or her foot. This activity is also fun to do with a group of your child's friends. Do two children have the same perimeters for foot or hand, but different areas?

Literature Connection

Spaghetti and Meatballs for All by Marilyn Burns

> Students in grades 3 to 5 should develop methods for estimating the measurements of perimeters, area, and volumes of irregular shapes.

Irregular shapes pose a problem for using traditional measuring tools. For example, can you measure the distance around a pumpkin using a ruler? Children need to develop their own methods for solving this problem. How about using a string around the pumpkin and then measuring the string with the ruler?

You can guide your child, but do not be too quick to tell him or her how to do it. Much of the learning takes place in the struggle to solve the problem. Finding the areas of irregular shapes can seem daunting to a child. For small shapes, tracing the shape onto grid paper and counting the squares can work. In the case of large areas, have your child divide the irregular area into rectangular and triangular parts, figure the area for each part, and then add.

Estimating Areas of Pictures

Materials
You will need some old magazines with a variety of different-sized pictures that your child can cut out, paper, a pencil, scissors, and 1-inch or 1-centimeter square grid paper (see the Appendix, pages 205–208).

Procedure
Choose a fairly large picture from a magazine. To help your child acquire skill at estimating area, discuss what he or she thinks would be the largest rectangle that would fit in the picture. Let's say the picture is of a car. Would a 4-by-6-inch (10-by-15-cm) rectangle cover the largest part of the car's body? Have your youngster figure that area. Then ask, "Could there be smaller rectangles used to figure the areas of the parts of the picture not covered by the large rectangle?" Maybe a 1-by-1-inch (2.5-by-2.5-cm) rectangle would cover the wheels, or a 1-by-2-inch (2.5-by-5-cm) rectangle would cover the roof and window parts. Have your child figure those areas. Then, have your child add the areas together. To see how close the estimate is to the actual measurement, your child can now cut out the picture and trace its outline onto a sheet of grid paper. He or she can count the squares inside the outline, including parts of squares. Have your child compare the original estimate to the grid count and see how close he or she came.

Area Estimation Scramble

This activity is a simple game requiring estimation and mental math skills. It is great practice for estimating quickly!

Materials

Use index cards cut into fourths to make playing cards with the numbers 21 through 40—just one number to a card. You should have two players for this game.

Procedure

The object of this game is to use the numbers on two of the playing cards as dimensions of a rectangle and, from those dimensions, to estimate the area of that rectangle. For example, the cards with the numbers 22 and 38 would result in an area of about 800 (20 × 40). Shuffle the cards and place the deck face down on the playing surface. Both players draw two number cards, not looking at what numbers they have drawn. The two numbers represent the dimensions of a rectangle. One player says, "Go," and both players turn their pair of cards up so that they both can see them. Both players quickly estimate the area for their pair of numbers and for their opponent's numbers. The players determine which pair has the greater area and then stand up. The player who stands up first and correctly names the greater area wins a point.

For most numbers, children should be able to use their number sense and estimating skills to make a quick mental decision. For instance, if one pair of numbers was the 22 and 38 previously mentioned, the players could round off the two and multiply them in their heads. If the other pair was 21 and 33, they might round one down to 20 and the other to 30—guessing an area of about 600. With some numbers, it would be obvious which has the greater area because one pair of numbers is much larger than the other. For example, 39 and 40 would be greater than 23 and 26.

In case of a disagreement over which pair is greater, players may figure the actual area by multiplying the two pairs or by using a calculator to do the computation. The first player with five points wins the game.

Perimeters and Gift Wrapping

Holidays and birthdays provide an enjoyable occasion to explore the perimeters of packages and boxes with different sizes and shapes.

Materials

You will need a variety of different-shaped packages or boxes. If you are actually wrapping presents, this is an especially meaningful experience. However, if your child is studying this concept in school, any supply of boxes or containers will do. You will also need string or ribbon, a measuring tool, and wrapping paper.

Procedure

Discuss the three different ways that string or ribbon could be put around a particular box.

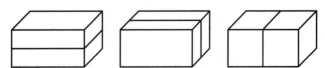

Have your child decide what the two longest sides are for the box, then what the two shortest sides are. He or she needs to make an estimate for the length of a short side and a long side. Review with your child how to find perimeters. (For a box, the distance around all four sides.) From this, he or she should be able to estimate how much ribbon it would take to go one way around the box. Your child can then estimate how much ribbon it would take to go the other two ways around the box. To check the estimate, put a piece of string around the box and then measure the string, laying it along the measuring tool. Which way would use the most ribbon? Which would use the least ribbon? You can then cut the ribbon to finish wrapping the gift.

Capacity Calculations

Since volume is the measurement of how much space an object holds or how much space it takes up, the estimation of unusual shapes can be a challenge. Children begin the study of volume by working with rectangular-shaped containers and figuring how many cubes it takes to fill them. This activity is not meant to have an exact answer. The exploration of possibilities is the aim.

Materials
All you will need are some balloons, different-sized boxes, rulers, a liquid measure, and an active imagination.

Procedure
The object of this activity is for your child to figure the volume of an inflated balloon. Begin by blowing up the balloon to about the size of a small cantaloupe. It is your child's task to figure a way to determine the balloon's volume. Don't let your child know right away, but here are some hints. Could another balloon be filled with water until it is the same size, and then the water poured out and measured? Could the balloon be crammed into a box and the box measured to figure the volume? Could the balloon be pushed into a full container of water sitting in a pan, and the displaced water that overflows be measured? Once again, the learning is in the exploring—trying one thing, and if that doesn't work, trying something else.

Literature Connection

Covering and Surrounding: Two Dimensional Measurement by Glenda Lappan, Elizabeth D. Phillips, James T. Fey, William M. Fitzgerald, and Susan N. Friel

Upper elementary students should choose and appropriately apply the standard units and tools to measure length, weight, area, volume, time, temperature, and the size of angles.

By third grade, children will be using some measuring tools, such as rulers, balance scales, clocks, and thermometers. At this level, children need to become more precise in their measurements—for example, making sure that the 0 on the ruler is lined up with the end of what they are measuring or that the balance scale is truly in balance. Third graders should be able to tell time to the nearest quarter hour, while fourth graders should tell time to the nearest minute. Children should be able to easily read and interpret thermometers whose scale is marked in increments of two.

Schools today introduce new units and tools in fourth and fifth grade. Children begin to measure circles and angles and to use a protractor. They perfect squared units for area and begin to learn cubic units for volume. By the end of students' elementary years, their basic measurement skills should be fairly well honed.

Measurement Match-Up

Materials

You and your child will need to make a set of cards. Index cards cut in half will work. There are three different types of cards. Write the names of objects to measure on one type (or you can use pictures). Write the names of measurement tools on the second type. Write measurement units on the third type. You should have two players for this game.

Objects to Measure: the temperature of food on the stove, when to go to school, how long until your birthday, how long it takes to wash your face, the length of your pencil, the length of a piece of paper, the length of your index finger, the distance to the next town, the distance to Los Angeles, the length of your bedroom, the length of your backyard, the distance a paper airplane flies, the amount of soda you drink from a glass, the amount of milk a family drinks at dinner, the amount of gasoline in the car, the weight of an apple, the weight of a crayon, the weight of a textbook, the weight of a cat.

Measurement Tools: thermometer, clock, calendar, balance scale, platform or kitchen scale, bathroom scale, measuring cup, yardstick, meter stick, inch ruler, centimeter ruler, odometer, metal measuring tape, gallon bottle, liter measure, watch, cloth measuring tape.

Measurement Units: inch, centimeter, foot, decimeter, yard, meter, mile, kilometer, cup, pint, quart, gallon, liter, ounces, pounds, gram, kilogram, second, minute, hour, day, week, month, degree.

Your upper grade child should be able to make the cards. It is helpful to color code the cards, making all the "Object" cards one color, the "Tool" cards a second color, and the "Unit" cards a third color.

Procedure

Turn one card of each type face up between two players. Shuffle the rest of the stack and deal the cards. The object of the game is to match an "Object," "Tool," and "Unit" card to make a complete set. One player begins by laying one of the cards in his or her hand down on top of one of the upturned cards on the playing surface to make a match. For instance, if "how long until your birthday" (an "Object" card), "yardstick" (a "Tool" card), and "hour" (a "Unit" card) are turned up, the player could play the "calendar" card in his or her hand on the "how long until your birthday" card because a calendar is the tool needed to figure the answer. It is then the second player's turn. If he or she has one of the "Unit" cards "day," "week," or "month," he or she can play it, making a complete set of "Objects," "Tools," and "Units." That player picks up the set, scoring five points. He or she then replaces the "Object" card with one from his or her hand. If he or she has no card to make the replacement, the other player may replace it with one from his or her hand. If the second player cannot complete a set, he or she may play on either of the other two upturned cards. It is then the first player's turn. Play continues until no more matches can be made or a player plays all of his or her cards. Being able to play all your cards also earns five points for the player. Tally all the points. The winner is the player with the highest score.

Literature Connection

The Math Chef: Over 60 Math Activities and Recipes for Kids by Joan D'Amico
The 100-Pound Problem by Jennifer Dussling

> Children of this age group should be able to choose and use a known quantity to help them estimate other measurements.

Students in grades 3 to 5 have now been working with measurement for several years and should have a feel for certain quantities. They may know that their height is about 5 feet (1.5 m), so they can estimate that the height of their bedroom door is about 7 feet

(2.1 m). Or they may know that one tile on the floor is 9 inches (22.5 cm) long, so by counting the number of tiles in the width of the floor and multiplying by nine, they can find the overall width.

Another skill in estimation of measurements is to decide when it is appropriate to overestimate and when to underestimate. If a child is estimating how long it will take to get to his or her best friend's birthday party, it may be wise to overestimate, or the child could be late. Similarly, if cooking, it may be good to underestimate the cooking time so that the child and parent do not burn the food.

There are many strategies for estimating measurements, and the one used will vary with the particular situation. You, as an adult, apply these automatically with little thought. Kids need a variety of experiences in order to carefully judge which strategies work in different situations.

Using Paces to Estimate

The common practice of pacing off a distance is well known to adults as an estimation technique. Teach this to your child to reinforce using a quantity he or she knows to estimate measurement.

Materials
You will need a measuring stick (either yard or meter), paper, a pencil, and a calculator (optional).

Procedure
It is great to teach this skill outdoors. Point out an object in the distance and ask your child to estimate how far it is between where he or she is standing and the object. Then, explain that there is a better way to estimate than just guessing, and that this is by using his or her pace. To figure the length of space, have your child take two normal paces forward. Measure the distance from where he or she started. Divide the measurement by two to get an average single pace. Your child can now pace off the distance to the object in the distance, counting the number of paces. Your child should then multiply the number of paces by the length of his or her pace. Fourth and fifth graders may need help, or they can use a calculator for the division and multiplication.

Many children are intrigued and delighted by this discovery and will want to try it out on other objects.

Larger than a Blue Whale?

Here is another activity that combines literature and math.

Materials

You will use the book *Is a Blue Whale the Biggest Thing There Is?* by Robert E. Wells as the basis for this activity. You will also need a ruler and tape measure.

Procedure

Read the book with your child. This book provides a look at the size of things that exist in the world. It begins by showing the largest animal on earth, the 100-foot- (30.5-m-) long blue whale. Have your child estimate how many lengths of his or her height would equal the length of an adult blue whale. You may need to demonstrate using multiples of your own height—for example, "I'm 6 feet tall. Two of me would be 12 feet . . ."

After your child has made the estimate, find a spot outdoors and use the tape measure to actually measure off 100 feet. Figure the number of lengths of your child's height there would be in the 100 feet. Was your child's estimate close?

You and your child can draw a picture to show the relationship of your child's height to the length of the whale. Your child, and probably you as well, will be amazed at how large an animal the blue whale really is.

You can do the same activity using other objects in comparison to the blue whale. For example, how many car lengths would it take? How many lengths of your house?

Literature Connection

Is a Blue Whale the Biggest Thing There Is? by Robert E. Wells
What's Smaller than a Pygmy Shrew? by Robert E. Wells

> **Older students should discover, understand, and apply formulas in order to find the area of rectangles, triangles, and parallelograms.**

Schools today first teach finding the area of rectangles by drawing the shape on grid paper. Children find the area by counting the number of squares that are inside the shape. Likewise, children find the areas of triangles using a grid system, but with the added understanding that sometimes there are only half squares inside the triangle. Students learn to put two halves together to make one square unit and figure the area. With parallelograms, children make a new discovery: this shape is made of both a rectangle and triangles.

In the upper grades, children should begin to see patterns to finding area and begin to understand formulas as we know them. With familiarity in finding area, children realize that it is not necessary to always divide a shape into small squares and count. A rectangle's area can be found by multiplying its two dimensions: length times width equals area, or A = L × W.

Children also discover formulas for finding the area of triangles (½ B × H).

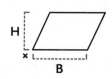

For parallelograms, the formula is similar to the one for a rectangle. Find the height of the parallelogram and multiply it by the length of the base (B × H).

Teachers do not initially give these formulas to students. Children are led into making the discoveries on their own by drawing, building, and manipulating shapes. Students often keep track of their discoveries about area by recording the information in a table. Then, they can readily see the number relationships and patterns.

Discovering Formulas

Formulas can always be taught by telling children, "Just use them. That's the way it is done." However, students will gain little understanding this way, and applying them in appropriate places becomes difficult.

Materials
You will need grid paper (see the Appendix, pages 205–208) and a pencil or pen for this activity.

Procedure
For rectangles, have your child draw them on grid paper. Then, your youngster can put the dimensions on one long side and one short side. An example might be for the child to draw a rectangle that is five squares across the top and four squares down the side. (The dimensions are a 5 × 4.) Then, have your child count all the squares inside the rectangle to find the area. (The area equals 20 squares.) After exploring many of these rectangles on grids, children soon make the connection that if they just multiply the dimensions, it always equals the squares inside. Thus, the formula L × W = A (length times width equals area) makes sense.

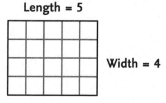

Your child can do the same thing with triangles. It may take more time to discover that the area is only half of the base times the height, but using the grid paper makes

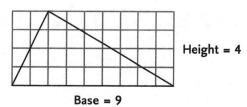

it visual. Even if you have to give hints to make the discovery, having the visual example will make it meaningful for your child.

Parallelograms also work well on grid paper. After your child has an exploration period, you may need to count all the inside squares and then demonstrate how multiplying the base and the height result in the same answer. Of course, your child should not work on parallelograms until he or she understands how the formula for rectangles works.

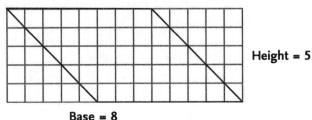

Area = 40 square units (8 × 5 = 40)

Height = 5

Base = 8

> In grades 3 to 5, students should develop methods to find the volumes and surface areas of rectangular solids.

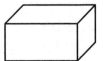

Finding the volume of a rectangular solid is an abstract idea that is difficult for many children to understand. Students have difficulty visualizing the number of cubic units it takes to build a solid, because often some of those cubes are in the center of the solid and cannot be seen. It is common for even older students to count only the cubes on the surface that they can actually see. When the concept of volume is introduced, children build rectangular prisms using blocks or cubes and then count the cubes. Kids need to build, build, build to prove to themselves that there need to be supporting cubic units in the center of the solid. Once this becomes established, the formula of volume—length times width times height ($V = L \times W \times H$)—makes sense. With enough practice making rectangular solids, children may come up with the formula on their own.

Surface areas of three-dimensional shapes pose a similar problem because children must find the area of many surfaces, including the base that the rectangular solid is sitting on. Here is another hidden area that is hard to visualize. Given practice and more practice, kids will create strategies for finding the surface areas of rectangular solids.

Building Models of Area and Volume

As stated throughout this book, doing, making, or building is the surest path to understanding. Making models requires linear measurement as well as learning about area and volume.

Materials

You will need old newspapers or other large sheets of paper, masking or transparent tape, rulers and meter sticks, scissors, cardboard, and markers or pencil or pen.

Procedure

After your child has been introduced to the concepts of area and volume, either at school or home, let him or her thoroughly explore their meaning by making models. Provide the materials, but give little instruction on how to do it. Simply tell your youngster to use the paper to measure, cut, and tape examples of shapes having a particular area or volume.

Here is a sample list of models to make:

Area Models (squares, rectangles)

1 square centimeter	12 square inches
10 square centimeters	1 square foot
8 square centimeters	2 square feet
1 square inch	1 square meter
4 square inches	1 square yard

Volume Models (cubes, prisms):

1 cubic centimeter	9 cubic inches
6 cubic centimeters	1 cubic foot*
1 cubic inch	1 cubic meter*

May need to be made from lightweight cardboard

To extend the concepts, have your child figure the surface area of the volume models he or she has made.

Write a Riddle

Kids love riddles. Some of the most poplar books in the school library are filled with them. In this activity, your child and a partner combine writing riddles with reviewing the measurement concepts of length, width, height, perimeter, surface area, and volume.

Materials

You will need paper, pencils, a ruler (either centimeter or inch), a measuring stick (either yard or meter), and index cards. You should have two players for this game.

Procedure

Your child and a partner will each list on paper the names of five objects in the room or house. Using the measurement tools, both players collect information about their objects, recording the data next to the name of each object. (Information includes length, width, height, perimeter, surface area, and, if applicable, volume.) After collecting the information, each person writes a riddle about the object on an index card using the data. They should do this for each object. The two players trade the riddles, and each person tries to solve the other person's riddle, guessing what the object is.

Variation

To increase difficulty, separate the two players into different rooms so that they cannot see what the other player is measuring.

Data Analysis and Probability

5

It has been said that we are living in the Information Age. Often, the information we receive today is obsolete within a year, and sometimes even by the following week. It is therefore essential that children be taught to collect information or data on their own, so that they can answer questions whose solutions are not rote or obvious. Because there is a glut of information out there, they also need to be able to analyze data to understand its meaning and validity. Of equal importance, children need to be able to make inferences and predictions from information in order to make decisions for themselves. To that end, children need to learn that they can gather information from a variety of places—not only from books, television, and the Internet, but also from various types of graphs, charts, and tables.

Once again, the best method for youngsters to learn these concepts is by doing. Children start making surveys, collecting data, and making graphs, charts, and tables using real objects as early as kindergarten. As they progress through the grades, their analysis of data and its representations becomes more and more sophisticated.

In terms of evaluating data, children also need to learn to make judgments about an event's probability of happening. In the lower grades, today's schools informally introduce children to the concepts through the playing of games that use spinners and dice. Upper grade students learn to make judgments about an event's chances of occurring as being likely or unlikely, or to give numerical odds for an event—for example, a 1-in-2 chance, or a probability of 50/50.

Children need to develop independent-thinking skills to successfully navigate the ocean of ever-changing data and information that has become part of our daily existence. Your child's ability to analyze data and probability is a necessary skill for him or her to become an independent thinker. You can be the guide to teach your child to question, evaluate information, make judgments, and think for him or herself. It is not necessary for you to have all the answers to your child's questions. It is all right to say, "I don't know. Let's find out." Make the quest for solutions with your child and teach by example.

Skills and Activities for Grades Pre-Kindergarten to 2

Children in the primary grades should learn to form questions and gather information or data about themselves and their environment.

As you well know, youngsters are just brimming over with questions, from, "Why is the sky blue?" to "How many red M&M's are in the bag?" Sometimes the question is just, "Why?" Parents should encourage this natural need to ask questions as children seek to learn about themselves and the world around them. To help youngsters become informed decision makers, parents need to teach them how to gather the information needed to answer questions lacking obvious solutions.

Posing Questions

While it is a natural inclination for children to question the world around them, they need to be directed as to how to ask questions that are specific and coherent. Both teachers and parents are important in developing this skill. When your child asks, "Why?" encourage him or her to ask in a complete sentence—for example, "Why do you want me to eat broccoli?" Stating questions in complete sentences causes the thinker to clarify what he or she really wants to know.

Children also need to be instructed and helped to make their questions more precise or detailed in order to gain the knowledge they seek. Instead of "What's that on the table?" a more specific question would be, "What is the large blue thing with yellow dots that is sitting on the table?" While these are everyday questions, and not particularly oriented toward data analysis, they teach your child how to ask questions clearly. If posing thoughtful questions at home becomes part of everyday life, the skill will easily transfer to the school setting and your child's ability to analyze data.

Young children should begin to analyze data by sorting and classifying objects by their properties and then organizing the information they have discovered about the objects.

One of the first skills toward analyzing data is being able to sort and classify objects by one or more properties. As discussed in chapter 2, "Algebra," sorting and classifying help children to make sense of information. It allows them to be able to see similarities and differences. Once children have sorted and categorized objects, they need to organize the objects so that they can make conclusions.

What's Really in a Bag of M&M's?

For the pre-k and kindergarten child, you should introduce sorting, classifying, and organizing informally in tasks such as putting toys away or putting the flatware in the proper place in the kitchen drawer. Children learn that certain things go together and others do not. For first and second grade students, the steps are more formalized.

Materials
You will need a small bag of multicolored candies (such as M&M's) as well as other small items to sort, such as spools of thread, animal crackers, wrapped hard candy, or coins.

Procedure
Have your child sort the candy pieces by color. After sorting, your child needs to organize the candy. One way is to line up each color group in a straight line and start from a common point. This makes it easy to see which color has the most and which has the least. The organization of the information makes the answers apparent.

Your child has just made a bar graph, using real objects!

Do you need other ideas for things to sort and organize? Try sorting spools of thread into reds, blues, greens, or yellows. How about sorting animal crackers? Or a sack of assorted wrapped hard candy? Maybe even a handful of coins? Your child can also arrange these into rows or columns to see which is more or less.

Literature Connection

The M&M's Brand Chocolate Candies Counting Board Book by Barbara Barbieri McGrath

Red   ● ● ●
Blue   ● ● ● ● ●
Green   ● ● ● ● ● ●
Yellow   ○ ○

> **Children in this age group should begin to represent the data they find by using real objects, pictures, and simple graphs.**

Today's schools introduce primary students to many methods for showing information. At the earliest levels, children use real objects, such as M&M's, animal crackers, Matchbox cars, and even kids' shoes or their teddy bears. They may begin by comparing only two groups—for example, chocolate chip cookies and sandwich cookies. They will count the number of each cookie type in a group. Children will also discuss how the two groups are alike and how they are different. As children become more experienced at representing data, you can substitute counters such as beans or buttons and pictures of real objects for actual objects to show information. By the end of second grade, children can explore simple graphs such as bar graphs and line plots.

At the kindergarten to first grade level, children do these investigations into representing data as whole class projects, with the teacher guiding the discussions and type of representations used for the information. As children mature, they may work in teams to make their graphs, charts, or tables. Then, the group reports to the class on what it did to collect the data, how it chose a particular representation, and what its information project shows.

Floor Graph

As previously stated, children begin graphing experiences by using real objects. One way to do this is by making a floor graph. This is a large grid that you can put on the floor for your youngster's use, as he or she organizes actual objects onto a graph. It helps your child keep the objects in each column aligned and starting from the same point. You can use it over and over to practice graphing in a variety of ways.

Materials

You can make the floor graph from many different materials—a plastic shower curtain or long vinyl tablecloth, a roll of shelf paper, or even an old sheet. Use a permanent marker to make the lines of the graph grid. Make the grid large enough to accom-

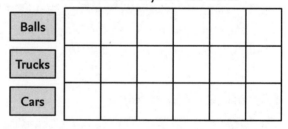

What Kind of Toys Do You Have?

modate a toy, a shoe, or a book. A two- or three-column grid is perfect for kindergarteners and first graders. Second graders may need a grid with five columns. The length of each column can vary—six to ten squares should be sufficient. You will need paper or index cards and markers or crayons for making labels and titles.

Procedure

You and your child can make labels from paper or index cards and place them at the beginning of each column. Then, all you need is a good question for your child to investigate and graph. An example might be: "Look at all your toys. What kinds of toy do you have?" Write the question on a long strip of paper and place it on top of the grid. This is the title of the graph. Make labels for each category of toy—for example, "Balls," "Trucks," and "Cars." Your child is now ready to gather up his or her toys, sort them into categories, and place them onto the grid—only one toy per box. Be sure that the toys are placed in the correct column. Discuss the results of the graph with your child. You can ask questions such as, "Which type of toy do you have the most of?" "Which type do you have the least of?" or, "How many more trucks do you have than cars?"

Some other ideas to graph using the floor graph are:

Types of books
Types of shoes (tie, buckle, slip-on)
Flatware in your kitchen drawer (knives, forks, spoons)
Types of stuffed animals (cats, dogs, bears)
Types of writing instruments (wooden pencils, mechanical pencils, pens)
Fruits in the refrigerator (apples, oranges, bananas)

Literature Connection

Bart's Amazing Charts by Dianne Ochiltree

> **Young children should learn to compare parts of the data displayed on graphs and tables (for example, "More first graders like chocolate ice cream than vanilla") and make conclusions about the data as a whole (for example, "Most of the students in the first grade class are six years old").**

Through many experiences involving collecting and organizing data, primary students discover that charts, graphs, and tables give information. At their level, much of the discovery about what a graph or table shows is done as a class discussion. Children are encouraged to look at different parts of the data shown on a graph and to make comparisons—for example, "There are the same number of red M&M's as brown ones" or, "There are more blue M&M's than red ones." Children elicit conclusions about the information that is shown by the whole graph or chart—for example, "More of the M&M's are green than any of the other colors."

By the end of second grade, students should begin to question erroneous conclusions that they draw from data—for example, "All bags of M&M's will have more blue ones than other colors." Children with experience in data collection and representation would know this might not be true.

Small Grid Graphing

Children can do many activities using much smaller grids and small packages of snacks containing a variety of morsels. Packages of trail mix or party mix are types of snacks that are perfect for this tasty graphing event.

Materials

You will need standard 1-inch grid paper (see the Appendix, page 208) for small objects. However, you may want to make a slightly larger grid on plain paper using 1½-inch or 2-inch squares. You will also need a pen or pencil, your favorite package of mixed snacks, glue, and crayons.

Procedure

At the top of the grid, write a title—for example, "What is the 'mix' in trail mix?" In the column of squares farthest to the left, have your child glue one of each type of morsel found in the bag. Your child should then sort the trail mix by morsel type and glue each one in the appropriate column. This results in a kind of bar graph. Again, you should ask questions about what the snack graph shows—for example, "Is there one type of morsel in the snack mix that there are more of than any of the others?" "Are there some types of snack that have the same amount?" or, "What is the most common snack in the mix? What is the least?"

To adapt this activity to older children in second grade, have them represent the different types of snacks using symbols. Instead of gluing the real objects onto the grid, they can make a pictograph by drawing a picture of the morsels in each square. To make a bar graph, your child can write the title or question that is being investigated, then label the first square with the name of the type of snack. He or she will count how many there are of each kind using tally marks and then color in a square for each one counted.

What Is in the Mix?

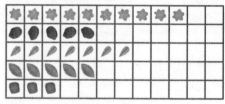

You might want to note that tally marks are often used to help count the different categories. The child writes the name or makes a picture of each type of snack in the bag. As your child sorts the contents, he or she should make a tally mark for each piece. As an example:

After the tallying is complete, your child makes the bar or pictograph. Tell your child to try not to eat the data before the tallying is done!

Pretzel	ＨＨ ＨＨ ///
Corn	ＨＨ ＨＨ
Wheat	ＨＨ ＨＨ ＨＨ
Rice	ＨＨ ///
Melba Round	ＨＨ /

Literature Connection

A Three Hat Day by Laura Geringer

> Primary students should begin to develop skills in making predictions and inferences by discussing events and experiences in their own lives in terms of being likely or unlikely to happen.

For young children, it is difficult to make inferences and predictions. These concepts are more suited to upper grade students. However, small children can discuss events that are in the realm of their experience as being likely or unlikely to happen—for example, "It is summertime. Will it be likely or unlikely to snow?" or, "It is lunchtime. Will it be likely or unlikely that I will have milk to drink?"

When playing games with your child, simply take a minute to ask what he or she thinks will have the best chance of occurring. In dice games using one die, does one number come up more often than another? Is the same true when using two dice and adding the two together? You, as an adult, know that, theoretically, one number on a die is no more likely to come up than another. However, in the short term, this may not be true. You could roll 4 three times in a row or never roll a 1. Let your child explore.

At first your child will not do well, often choosing his or her favorite number or thinking that if one number comes up more often in a limited number of rolls, it must be the most likely. It is OK for your child to be incorrect. The concepts of probability are developed through experience after experience. Just keep asking, "What do you think will happen?" or, "Did it happen the way you thought?"

Number Cube Tally

Materials
You will need a half sheet of paper (8½-by-5½ inches [21-by-14-cm]), a pencil, and a die or number cube.

Procedure
Help your child divide the paper into six boxes of equal size. He or she can then write the numerals 1 through 6, putting one numeral in each box. Have your youngster roll the die and record the number that it shows by putting a tally mark in the appropriate box. Limit the rolls to 20. Did one number come up more than the others? Did all the numbers come up the same number of times? Have your child repeat the activity and

compare the results. Were the results the same? Is there any number that is more likely or unlikely to come up in the 20 rolls? These are all questions to help lead your child into looking carefully at data. It is this type of activity that develops the concepts of probability that your child will formally study at an older age.

Literature Connection

No Fair! by Caren Holtzman

Skills and Activities for Grades 3 to 5

In the upper grades, students should design whole investigations: pose a question about themselves, their school, or their community; develop a plan to collect information; and evaluate how different methods of data collection affect the outcome.

Older students should formulate questions that involve themselves and their personal realm or issues and problems in their class, school, or community. Once they have formed a question, they should make a plan as to how to collect the data needed to answer the question. Students can collect their own data by making a survey or doing an experiment, or they may use existing data they find in written sources such as books, encyclopedias, newspapers, almanacs, and information found on the Internet.

As children are working, they may find they either need to refine their question by making it narrower or to broaden its scope. Make sure they address questions such as whom to ask, what to observe, where to make observations, and how to record the data.

Whew! What a job! That is exactly as it is supposed to be. By going through the whole process for data analysis and using a question that is meaningful to the child, real understanding of the whole process takes place. This isn't meant to be some 45-

minute math lesson or one hour of homework. This is a real project much like those many adults face in the workplace. The only difference is that it is at children's learning and interest level.

Did you realize your child worked this hard each day? Today's schools try to mirror the real world in many ways.

Survey Model of Data Analysis

Materials
You will only need some paper and a pencil or pen. You may also want some crayons or markers to add color to the graphs.

Procedure
Your child will need to develop a question that is appropriate for asking many people and conducting a survey. The question should be of interest to your child and have meaning for him or her. If sports are a favorite pastime, the question might be, "What is your favorite sport to play?" or, "What is your favorite sport to watch on TV?" or still, "What is your favorite NFL team?"

After deciding on a topic and question, you and your child should create a survey sheet with the question at the top, the choices listed down the side, and spaces next to each one to make tally marks for each person's response as well as the total tallies.

What is your favorite sport to play?

	Tallies	Total Number
Basketball		
Football		
Soccer		
Tennis		
Golf		

Now, it is time to do the survey. Your child should decide in advance how many people he or she will survey. Besides the number, it is important for your child to determine what types of people will be asked to participate. Will they all be children the same age as your child? Will children of different ages be asked? Will any adults be included? Your child should consider whether or not asking different groups of people the same question will change the results.

After the survey is concluded, your child should total the results for each category or answer choice and decide how best to present the results. Will the data best be shown by a bar graph, pictograph, circle graph, or a line plot?

Upon choosing a type of display for the data, be sure that your child places the question at the top, labels the categories, and uses numbers, so that all the information from the survey is easily apparent and can be interpreted.

Research Model of Data Analysis

Materials

You will need printed sources of facts and information, such as newspapers, encyclopedias, almanacs, or Internet sources. You will also need paper, pencils, and pens or markers for the graphing.

Procedure

Much of the process for asking a question that requires research is the same as for the survey model. It is still important that your child choose a question that appeals to him or her, or he or she will not be motivated to do the research. Let's say your youngster has an interest in weather. The question might be, "What is the average temperature for each month of the year in the place I live?"

Instead of creating a survey and asking people, your child collects data from printed sources. If your child collects each day's temperatures and averages them for each month, this could be a year's project. Sometimes it is possible to find the data for the year that has passed. Your child could develop a recording sheet to keep track of the data discovered, just as with a survey.

The rest of the process is the same as for the survey. Your child will need to make a decision as to which type of display will best show the information. Because the weather example is collecting data over time, a line graph is another possibility for presenting the results of the research.

Experiment Model of Data Analysis

Materials

For this exercise, you will need five different brands of bubble gum (or whatever product you decide to test), a clock or wristwatch, paper, pencils, pens, and markers or crayons for the graphic display.

Procedure

As with the other two models, experiments begin with a question. However, in this case, the information needed to answer the question is not found in a book or magazine or by talking with people. Instead, your child must perform a test. Just for fun, let's say your child wants to know which brand of chewing gum keeps its flavor the longest. In order to answer this question, he or she needs to devise and execute an experiment.

Have your child choose five brands of bubble gum. Your child will chew each brand until he or she can no longer detect any flavor. Using a clock or wristwatch, your child can record the time from when the gum is placed in his or her mouth until the flavor is gone. Your child will do this with all five brands. He or she might need to do it over five different sessions, since it could become difficult to tell when the flavors disappear if all the brands are done one after another. (Taste fatigue!)

As with all scientific experiments, all things should be kept as nearly alike as possible, except for the one variable: different chewing gum brands. Your child should chew all five brands, possibly all at the same time of day.

Once all the timed results are in from the experiment, your child will need to create a display to show what he or she has discovered. This is much the same as doing a survey or conducting research.

Literature Connection

NBA Math Skills: Slam and Jam by Scholastic Books

> **Children in grades 3 to 5 should learn to collect data by using observations, creating surveys, and conducting experiments.**

Upper grade students explore many ways to collect data. If they make observations, they learn skills for recording what they observe and how to organize it. With surveys, children may be taught techniques for sampling—for example, "Are we going to ask everyone in the class, five students in each grade, or only fifth graders?" Today's schools also teach students how to set up experiments by making a hypothesis, running tests or experiments, recording the data, and drawing conclusions.

Who Loves Pizza?

Does your child love pizza? Maybe he or she wonders what age group loves it the most. Here is a fun activity that uses a survey sampling several groups.

Materials
You will need paper and a pencil.

Procedure
First, have your child develop a question to ask people about how often they eat pizza—for example, "Did you eat any pizza during the last week?" After deciding which age groups to include in the survey, your child needs to create a survey sheet to record people's responses. He or she should also determine how many of each age group will be

surveyed. How about 10? Would anything change if 20 people were asked? A sample survey sheet is at right.

Conducting this survey will show that results may differ depending upon whom you ask.

Also, changing a question slightly may produce different results. If the question were rewritten to simply, "Do

Lovers of Pizza

Age Groups	Tally	Number of Yeses
Elementary Age		
Teens		
College Age		
Adults, 21 to 30		
Adults, 31 and up		

you like pizza?" would the results change? That, of course, would require a whole new recording sheet and survey to find out.

Let your child explore using different groups and a variety of questions.

Best Popcorn Buy

Almost everybody loves popcorn! It is delicious, healthy, and cheap. But which brand is really the best buy? Could a person find the information by doing a survey or making observations? Or would an experiment be the best method for finding the answer as to which brand is best? All experiments start with a question, and then your child must develop a plan as to how to find the answer. He or she poses a possible hypothesis or answer to the question—for example, Brand X is the best buy according to quantity versus cost. Your child then formulates a plan as to how to test the hypothesis. Then, he or she runs tests in order to prove or disprove the hypothesis. The most critical part of any experiment is keeping all aspects of each test the same, except for the one variable that is being tested.

Materials
You will need three to five different brands of popcorn, measuring cups and spoons, oil, a popcorn popper, paper, and a pencil.

Procedure
In this case, the variable is different brands of popcorn. Your child should carefully measure the same amount of corn for each brand, use the same amount of oil, and heat the same popper to the same temperature. Then, you and your child can pop and measure each brand of popcorn. The brand producing the most popped corn would be the best buy, provided that the costs per brand were similar. To make this a true experiment, your child should record data as to brands, amount unpopped, and amount popped for each. Once your child has collected the data using the scientific method described, he or she can display the data with a graph of his or her choice. Then, your child can eat the experiment!

> Children of this age group should learn to represent data they have collected using tables and graphs such as bar graphs, pictographs, line graphs, and line plots.

Once children collect data, they need to organize and show it. Children learn the differences between each of the various tables and graphs. They learn to make decisions about which representation would be best to show the particular data collected or a certain aspect of the data.

Another Way to Show Me

Materials
The primary thing you will need for this activity is an already-prepared graph or table. Those found in newspapers, magazines, or advertisements will do. You will also need paper, grid paper, a pencil, and colored markers or crayons.

Procedure
Discuss with your child the information shown on the prepared graph. Once you feel that your child understands the data, have him or her show the same information using a different type of display. Your child may use a bar graph (either horizontal or vertical), a circle graph, a pictograph, a line graph, a table, or a line plot. Explore with him or her how, if at all, the change in the display makes the data appear differently.

Better or Worse

Materials
You will need a collection of old books, magazines, and newspapers containing graphs or tables. Sometimes old textbooks are a good bet.

Procedure
Have your child search through periodicals, finding a variety of different types of graphs, charts, and tables. Discuss with him or her the advantages and disadvantages of each type. Talk about what types of information each best represents. Did you find any displays used for advertising that were efforts to influence your thinking?

Students of this age group should be able to compare and describe important features of data that are represented, such as *range* (least amount to the greatest amount), where data are clumped together, categories where there are no data, and areas that appear to have unusual values.

In the primary grades, students only make general conclusions about what a table or graph shows—for example, "Chocolate ice cream was the first grade class' favorite flavor." By grades 3 to 5, the analysis becomes much more particular. If students were looking at temperature data for the month of April, they might discuss the range—for example, "The range of temperatures was a minimum of 45 degrees and a maximum of 82 degrees." They would also consider other observations of the data—for example, "Most of the temperatures were concentrated around 65 degrees. There were no temperatures at 50 degrees. 82 degrees was an exception compared to the rest of the data." How data falls on a graph is called the **shape of the graph**.

Questions That Analyze Graphs

Children need to be taught how to look critically at information they see and hear. The following is a list of possible questions that you can ask them when they examine graphs or charts.

- What is the graph claiming?
- Is it possible to tell the method used to collect the data (for example, survey, research, or experiment)?
- How is the graph constructed?
- Does the graph use statistics correctly, or are they misused? (For example, was a general statement made that seemed to represent a large group, but only a small or select group was actually polled?)
- What is the graph not telling us that might change its interpretation?
- Does the graph present information in a clear form, or would a different display have been better?
- Are there other questions that could be asked about the information?

What Are the Odds?

Materials
You will need two dice, each numbered 1 to 6, paper, a pencil, and crayons or markers. You should make a recording sheet to tally results of rolling the dice. The sheet needs

to have the numbers 1 to 12 down one side and room for the tallies beside each number. Your child will use the frequency column to show the total number of tallies for each sum.

Procedure

Have your child roll the dice 20 times, tallying the sum of each roll. Then, ask him or her if the data seems to cluster around particular numbers. What is the range of sums rolled? Are there any sums that seem particularly infrequent? Those are called **outliers**.

This simple activity explores range, clusters, and outliers and helps to teach each concept. Now, have your child use these statistical terms when viewing other graphs or charts—with those constructed or presented in this chapter and with graphs found in newspapers or magazines.

To extend the activity, your child may graph the results of the dice rolls using the tallies and making a display with a bar graph. Do the activity a second time, or another 20 rolls. Were the results identical? Your

How Often Does Each Number Come Up?

Sum of Dice	Tally	Frequency
1		
2		
3		
4		
5		
6		
7		
8		
9		
10		
11		
12		

child can graph a second bar for each number on the same grid using a different color for the second set of data (a double bar graph). Can the two sets of data be analyzed? If they were not identical, were they similar? Was the range the same? Did the data from the second try cluster in the same way?

> Students in grades 3 to 5 should explore *mean* (average), *median* (exact center of a set of data), and *mode* (the most frequent member in a set of data). They should learn what each does and does not show about a set of data.

Let's explore the data for the number of e-mails received each day for a week: Sunday = 5, Monday = 3, Tuesday = 8, Wednesday = 5, Thursday = 4, Friday = 6, and Saturday = 7.

To find the mean, add all seven days of e-mails together and divide by 7. (5 + 3 + 8 + 5 + 4 + 6 + 7 = 38; divide 38 by 7 = 5.43.) The mean, or average, is 5.43.

To find the median, put the data in order from least to greatest and find the middle (3, 4, 5, 5, 6, 7, 8). The median is 5.

To find the mode, find the number that comes up most frequently. In this case, the mode is also 5 because it appeared twice and the other numbers only had one entry.

Discovering the Mean (Average), Median, and Mode

Materials
You will need a yardstick, paper, a pencil, and a calculator.

Procedure
The following are some ideas to provide your child with practice in figuring the three measures of center: mean, median, and mode. Have your child calculate all three for each activity.

Have your child find the height of each family member in inches. He or she should figure the mean for the family by adding all the heights and dividing by the number of people in the family. For a little practice in making measurement conversions, have your child change the inches into feet and inches. He or she can calculate the median and the mode, if there are enough people involved. To increase the amount of data, your child can include members of the extended family.

If your child likes to play a particular game—card, computer, or board games—record the score for the same game over a period of time. Depending upon how often your child plays the game, it could be for a week, a month, or, if it is a real favorite, daily. There should be at least five or more scores accumulated. Then, have your child calculate all three measures of center.

Have your child keep track of how many minutes a day he or she watches television (or plays computer games) for a week. Have your child find the daily mean. Extend the duration of the activity to a month and have your child figure the median and mode.

If you have access to a weather map showing temperatures for your state (or the United States), have your child figure the mean temperature. What was the median and mode? Many newspapers have excellent weather maps, as does the Internet.

Many examples from your daily routine may lend themselves to finding mean, mode, or median. Look for any situation where at least five to ten numbers are involved. Kids are fascinated with finding these measures of center, particularly if they can use a calculator, which is a great way to combine learning measures of center and calculator practice.

> Students of this age group should explore different ways to show the same data (for example, a table with tally marks, a bar graph, or a line plot) and evaluate how well each method shows important segments of the data.

Using data in centimeters about the length of fourth graders' feet, have your child note how using different representations emphasize certain aspects.

Do you see how simply changing the scale on the bar graphs for the number of children makes the differences in the categories shown by the bars appear differently? The first graph with a scale interval of one makes it seem as if there is a much larger difference in the number of kids than if you look at the last graph using five as its interval on the scale. This should help explain to your child how statistics get distorted.

LINE PLOT

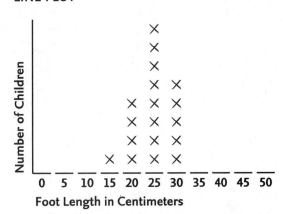

TABLE WITH TALLY MARKS

Foot Length Data

Length	Number of Children
15 cm	/
20 cm	////
25 cm	## ///
30 cm	##

BAR GRAPHS

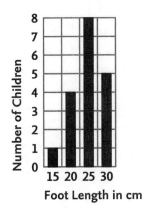

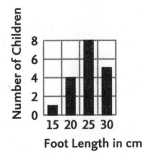

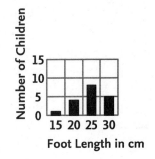

Brand X or Brand Y?

Remember the Pepsi Challenge? With this activity, your child will make a similar survey and graph the results in three ways.

Materials

You will need lined paper for the survey. You will also need plain paper, grid paper for graphing the survey data, and a pencil or crayons and markers.

Procedure

Your child will choose two like products to use for his or her survey—for example, regular cola or diet cola; pepperoni pizza or mushroom pizza; basketball or baseball; or any other somewhat related pair of choices. On the lined paper, your child will design a survey similar to the one at right.

Your child will now poll 20 people—friends, family, and neighbors. Each person polled will answer both questions by writing either "Yes" or "No" under each "Question" column. After the survey is complete, your child is ready to total the information, creating four data sets: (1) those people who liked both and therefore answered yes on both questions, (2) those who liked pepperoni, (3) those who liked mushroom, and (4) those who liked neither type of pizza.

Now, your child is ready to show the data using three different types of displays. First, he or she should show the data using a bar graph on grid paper, with the categories at the bottom and the number of people, 1 to 20, on the vertical axis, or left side. Then, your child should show the same data by using a circle graph and writing the categories in the appropriate section, using a fraction to show the number of people. As a third display, your child could represent the data using a Venn diagram. An example of a Venn diagram is shown below.

Your child should then analyze each type of representation and discover that the differences in the displays stress different information. For instance, the bar graph actually shows some people's responses twice, because those who answered yes to both questions will be tallied with each individual question and with the "Both" category. The Venn diagram better represents that overlap of data by showing the "Both" category in the center. What other differences can your youngster find?

SURVEY FORM

Please answer Yes or No to both questions.
Question 1: *Do you like pepperoni pizza?*
Question 2: *Do you like mushroom pizza?*

Person Polled	Question 1	Question 2
1		
2		
3		
4		
5		
6		
7		
8		
9		
10		
11		
12		
13		
14		
15		
16		
17		
18		
19		
20		

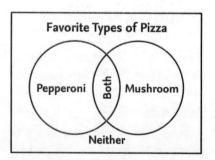

Favorite Types of Pizza

Pepperoni — Both — Mushroom

Neither

In grades 3 to 5, students should learn to make conclusions and predictions, justifying them based on a set of data. They also learn to create further investigations of their conclusions or predictions.

All this collecting of data and representing it on tables and graphs doesn't have much use unless kids can derive some meaning from them. Children should be encouraged to make predictions from their data. For instance, referring back to the temperature data for April, your child might predict that he or she should wear a jacket to school in the month of April. When asked to justify his or her reason, your child could use the data that shows most of the temperatures were clustered around 65 degrees, which is cool enough for a jacket.

Your child could plan further investigations into temperatures—for example, "How many days in April did I actually need to wear a jacket to school?" or, "What would the temperature data look like for May?"

Who's the Coolest?

Children in the upper grades often study regions of the United States as part of social studies. They learn to read maps, explore different climates, and examine regional economics affected by climate. The following activity not only has kids analyzing data and drawing conclusions as a mathematical study, but will also reinforce social science concepts.

Materials
You will need weather maps of the United States showing temperature and precipitation as a source for gathering data. Many newspapers carry weather maps and data. There are also excellent Web sites showing many weather maps that list temperature, precipitation, wind, and so on. You will also need paper for organizing the data—plain and grid—and a pencil or pen.

Procedure
Have your child divide the United States into five regions: northeast, south, central, southwest, and west. Have your child choose a major city in each region and make a recording sheet listing the cities down the side and the temperature ranges across the top of the columns.

Your child may need to adjust the temperature ranges for the season of the year. An example of a recording sheet might look like this:

Temperatures for Regions of the United States

City	20s	30s	40s	50s	60s	70s	80s	90s	100s
Boston									
Atlanta									
Omaha									
Phoenix									
Sacramento									

Your child can collect data over a certain period of time—a week or a month—using tally marks. What conclusions can your child make about what people's lives may be like in each region?

Your child can make another chart tracking precipitation in each city. Ask your child what conclusions he or she can draw from this set of data. If your child kept both charts, can any conclusions be drawn about agriculture, types of housing, or people's leisure activities? Is further information or data needed to answer those questions? Can predictions be made as to what the temperature or precipitation might be for the next week or month?

Now that your child has gone through the whole process, see if he or she can make predictions and draw conclusions from other charts, tables, and graphs. Does your child have good reasons for his or her predictions, or are they wild guesses? It is important for your child to realize that his or her statements should be based on the data and valid information, not just what he or she wishes would happen.

> Upper grade students should begin to learn that probability is a measurement of the likelihood of an event occurring and to use the terms *certain, equally likely,* and *impossible* to describe that probability.

Students in the lower grades have dealt with probability in generalities as it relates to their daily activities and experiences. Children in grades 3 to 5 begin to collect data about an event before making a statement about its probability of occurring. For instance, a fourth grader might want to know the probability of getting to play a favorite game in physical education. He or she could collect data for a month, finding the game was played only on Fridays. The child then could say he or she was certain it would be played every Friday. The child could also say that the likelihood of the game being played on Wednesday was impossible.

Predict the Outcome

Using this activity will help your youngster understand the possibilities of the terms *certain, equally likely,* and *impossible.*

Materials
You will need five small objects that are identical in every way except for color, such as buttons, game chips, beans, or the like. Four of the objects should be the same color (for example, black) and one object should be a different color (for example, white). You will also need a small, opaque bag.

Procedure
Allow your child to see all five objects. Place the four like objects in the bag, keeping the one different object out. Show him or her the one you kept out. Ask your child to predict what color object he or she will be able to draw out of the bag. In this instance, of course he or she will predict black. Tell your child that this is a certain prediction because it is the only possible answer. Have your youngster then predict the possibility of drawing a white object out of the bag. Your child will say he or she can't draw out a white one. This makes the possibility impossible. Easy, right? Your child will think so, too, but you have taught important vocabulary and set the stage for more difficult concepts involving prediction.

Now, put all the objects in the bag. Once again, ask your child to make a prediction as to what he or she is likely to pull out of the bag. You may wish to discuss that the choices of "certain" and "impossible" are no longer an option, since both black and white objects are in the bag. Hopefully, your child will say that black is most likely to be picked because there are more of them in the bag.

Now, add three more white objects to the bag and have your child choose a possibility. Through experiment and discussion, lead your child to understand that, for any one draw, the possibility is equally likely because the same number of each color is in the bag. Does that mean that they will be drawn equally? You and I both know that isn't always the case, but the probability is equal.

After you have completed this activity, look for opportunities in your everyday world to ask your child to make predictions about the likelihood of an event happening. Use the vocabulary *certain, possible, likely, equally likely,* and *impossible.*

Literature Connection
Jumanji by Chris Van Allsburg

Through spinner and dice games, older students are expected to analyze the probability of a particular outcome. Examples of different spinners show how probability can vary.

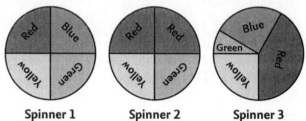

Spinner 1   **Spinner 2**   **Spinner 3**

As you can see on Spinner 1, the probability of red coming up is equal to the other three colors, or it has a 1-in-4 chance.

Spinner 2, while still divided into four equal parts, has a 2-in-4 probability of coming up red.

Spinner 3 has all four colors, but they are not of equal size. However, red still has the greatest probability of occurring.

Students learn to analyze these types of differences using both dice and spinners and by doing simple experiments.

Making a prediction about the probability of a particular number occurring on a spinner is called **theoretical probability**. In theory, red should come up on Spinner 2 half of the time.

But you and I know that in real life that does not always happen in the short term. (Ever been to Las Vegas or Atlantic City?) You cannot expect red to be the winner every other spin. What actually does happen is called **experimental probability**. In school, your child will play many probability games, recording each turn of a spinner or roll of dice to see if what theoretically should happen matches what actually does take place.

With any game involving chance that your family plays, you can reinforce probability concepts with a little discussion that encourages making predictions and seeing what happens.

Crossing the River

Materials

You need to make a simple game board with a double line across the middle to represent the river and docks on both sides of the river numbered 2 to 12 (see the diagram on the next page). Each player also needs a set of 12 "boats." The boats should all be of the same color for a single player, but a different color than an opponent's. You could use 12 white buttons for one player and 12 black buttons for the other, for example. To make it really simple, you could use paper squares of two different colors. You will also need two dice each numbered from 1 to 6, a sheet of grid paper for each player, and pencils. One-inch grid paper (see the Appendix, page 208) works best, but any size will do. You should have two players for this game.

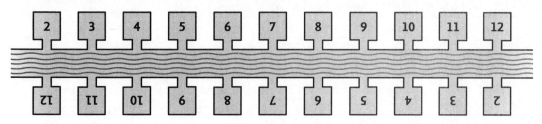

Procedure

Using the grid paper, each player should construct a blank graph to record the sum of the two dice he or she rolls. The graph should have the title "Crossing the River," and under that the question, "What number was rolled each turn?" Each player should write the numbers 2 through 12 in the bottom row of squares, one number to a square to represent the dock numbers. Each should also write the numbers 1 to 10 in the left-hand vertical row of squares to represent the number of times a number was rolled.

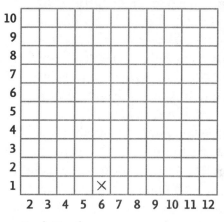

The object of the game is to get all 12 "boats" from their docks on one side of the river over to the other side. To start the play, each player puts his or her boats into any dock on his or her side. There can be no boats in one dock, all the boats in another dock, or any combination of boats per dock. The skill is in figuring the probability of which number will come up the most often, so that a player can place his or her 12 boats to the best advantage. Boats get to cross the river when the two dice are rolled and the sum of the two adds up to the number of a dock. For instance, the first player rolls a 6 and a 1. The sum is 7, so if he or she has a boat in Dock 7, the boat can cross the river. Only one boat may cross per roll. If a sum is rolled and there is no boat in that dock, the player loses a turn. Besides moving a boat to the other side, players record each sum of the two dice on the graph by coloring in a square. In our example, the first player would color in the square just above the 7. It is now the second player's turn to roll. Play continues until one player is able to move all of his or her boats across the river. The graph that is filled in with each roll becomes data that will allow the player to better predict where to place his or her boats for the next game.

Literature Connection

23 Super-Fun Math Spinner Games by Judi Aronson

> Children of this age group should learn to represent the measure of the likelihood that an event will happen by using a scale from 0 to 1; 0 represents impossible odds, 1 denotes a certain event, and a fraction between 0 and 1 represents probability for an event that is neither impossible nor certain.

Older students begin measuring probability by naming a particular number or by color out of the total possibilities. For instance, in the spinners previously discussed, children would measure the probability of red coming up on Spinner 1 as being 1-in-4 and Spinner 2's chances as being 2-in-4 (or 1-in-2).

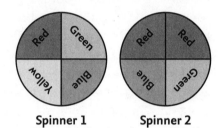

Spinner 1   **Spinner 2**

Once your child understands this concept well, he or she can represent probability measures by a fraction from 0 to 1. Once again using Spinner 2 as an example of color probability, yellow has 0 probability, blue and green have ¼, or 25 percent, probability of happening, and red has ½, or 50 percent, chance of occurring.

Spin a Color

With this activity, your child will explore the concepts of probability. The predictions of probability that your child makes will be expressed using 0, 1, or a fraction in between.

Materials

You will need several sheets of paper, a pencil, a ruler, crayons or markers, scissors, and a paper clip.

Procedure

Your child will construct several spinners, each divided into 10 equal parts. He or she can draw his or her own, or trace the one in the Appendix (see page 221).

To begin with, your child will make four spinners, coloring the number of pieces according to the following directions:

Spinner 1: 10 purple

Spinner 2: 2 purple, 2 brown, 2 white, 2 yellow, 2 pink
(or any five colors of your choice)
Spinner 3: 5 purple, 2 brown, 1 white, 1 yellow, 1 pink
Spinner 4: 4 purple, 3 brown, 2 white, 1 yellow

To finish making the spinners, have your child cut out each one and make a small hole in the center. Put one end of a paper clip around the hole, placing the point of the pencil through the paper clip and in the hole. The paper clip is the spinner.

Your child is now ready to explore probability with spinners. Have your child make a recording sheet for each spinner similar to the one below.

For each spinner, your child will predict the number of times that he or she thinks each color will occur out of 100 spins, writing the prediction as a fraction. (It is also possible to write the predictions based on 10, since there are 10 sections to the spinner.) If it is certain that a particular color will come up for every spin, the prediction is written as "1." If it is impossible for a particu-

Spinner 1

Prediction	Color	Tally	Total
	Purple		
	Brown		
	White		
	Yellow		
	Pink		

lar color to come up, the prediction is "0." After your child has made the prediction, he or she will spin the spinner 100 times and use tally marks to record which color occurs for each spin. Your child then totals the tallies. Did the prediction (based on theoretical probability) match the actual (or experimental) probability? Have your child try the exploration for Spinners 2, 3, and 4.

Your child should begin to see that the theoretical probability is based on the number of pieces that a certain color has on the spinner out of all the pieces. On Spinner 2, 2-in-10 is the probability expressed as $^2/_{10}$, or $^{20}/_{100}$.

To extend the activity, your child may wish to make other spinners, coloring the sections in a different arrangement. Your child may also wish to explore the relationship between his or her predictions and what actually occurred. If the experimental probability is quite different from the prediction, would he or she be closer after 200 or 500 spins?

Literature Connection

Do You Want to Bet? by Jean Cushman

Process Standards

The first five standards discussed in this book are the NCTM's Content Standards: Numbers and Operations, Algebra, Geometry, Measurement, and Data Analysis and Probability are the mathematical operations that children need to know. These areas contain the facts of mathematics. Learning how to multiply, measure to the quarter inch, or recognize two-dimensional shapes are important skills for kids to understand and be able to use.

The Content Standards, however, would be useless if kids did not know how, when, where, and why to apply them. What is the point of kids knowing how to do long division if they cannot recognize situations when it is appropriate to do so?

For this reason, the last five standards are called Process Standards. These five areas are what children need to do in order to learn to think and reason mathematically. The Process Standards are Problem Solving, Reasoning and Proof, Communication, Connections, and Representation. Each standard will be discussed in depth in the subsequent five chapters.

The format in these last five chapters will differ slightly from the chapters about the Content areas. The NCTM states that only one set of skills applies to pre-kindergarten through fifth grade, instead of having separate skills for primary and upper grades. Of course, the application level of difficulty varies from primary to upper grades. As in the earlier chapters, recommendations for activities or practice strategies will be given for each age group. Although the listed activities have been used previously in the Content chapters, they will now be looked at from a different perspective, revealing how children's learning experiences are multilayered. This will help you understand the aim behind teaching your child the Process Standards.

Problem Solving

Problem solving is an essential part of the human condition. As an adult, you begin solving problems as soon as the alarm goes off in the morning, and you finish when your day is done. True, most of these problems are small, but every grown-up faces, at some time, problems that require a variety of strategies to solve.

Small children are naturals at problem solving because everything in the world is new to them. They are full of curiosity and, often, perseverance. Have you ever watched a toddler try to reach an object on the far side of the table? At first, the youngster keeps reaching and reaching. He or she may try to climb in order to get closer. The child may move partway around the table and try again. Finally, he or she makes the connection to walk around the table to get on the same side as the object. Success—object reached! The problem was solved by trial and error, plus a lot of persistence—a quality to be nurtured as children mature.

While problem solving is found in all areas of our lives and at school in many subjects, the focus of this chapter is how problem solving relates to mathematics. For our purpose, problem solving gives kids a chance to use what they have learned in the Content areas of math and extend what they already know into new areas. If you look back at the majority of activities listed in the chapters on Content Standards, the math skills taught are set in a problem-solving context. Kids understand and remember when they "do," instead of just memorizing.

Problem solving is the basis for mathematics in today's schools. If kids do not have the ability to solve problems, the math skills they learn are essentially useless. Children who can create a plan and implement it to solve a mathematical problem show a much greater understanding of math than kids who can simply add, subtract, multiply, and divide.

There are four main objectives for elementary students, pre-kindergarten through fifth grade, under the Problem-Solving standard:

Students should learn new mathematical skills and ideas through the problem-solving process.

Problem solving not only gives math skills meaning, but it also is a path to learning new skills and ideas in the field. Third graders trying to find the average height of the students in their class engage in the Content skills of measuring, adding, and dividing. Children of this age group can measure and add, but division is new to them. Through problem solving, they are introduced to division and its meaning, even if they must do the computation on a calculator. The problem-solving context makes division understandable.

Children should solve problems not only in mathematics, but also in other subjects and areas of their lives.

While the main focus for problem solving may be in a mathematical context, the process should also be used in other subject areas, such as science and social studies. Ultimately, it is hoped that children will be able to transfer and use this process, not only at school, but also in all areas of their lives.

Elementary students should learn and apply a variety of strategies to solve problems.

In the past, problem solving in school was basically the dreaded story problem. If you were like most students of your age group, the only strategy you were left with was to stare at the paper in front of you and hope that, if you did that long enough, the solution would magically appear.

Today, strategies for problem solving are much more defined. There are a variety of strategies that students learn, and, through practice, they can discover which strategy may work best with a certain type of problem. These particular strategies will be discussed in detail later in this chapter.

> **Children should learn to think about the problem-solving processes they use and to communicate their thoughts to others.**

Kids are encouraged to think about their thinking. "What exactly was going on in your mind as you solved this problem?" "What were the steps you went through?" and, "What did you do to get the solution?" are examples of the types of questions that promote thinking about the problem-solving process. Having children reflect on the steps increases their understanding of the process. Communicating those steps, either orally or in written form, basically forces that reflection and makes the thinking more precise.

You may be asking at this point, "What is my role in helping my child become a problem solver?" The most important thing that you can do is foster an environment in which your child is not afraid to take risks. In problem solving, children need to feel free to explore, try something new, and even risk being wrong. While the objective is to find the solution, making a mistake is OK. This comes with praise for trying and respect for their acceptance of the challenge of new territory. Your goal is to give your child the security needed to venture into finding solutions.

Problem solving also requires time to think. As you probably know from dealing with your own problems, solutions are not always instantaneous. Do not be too eager to give the answer. Strong problem solvers are allowed to struggle, make mistakes, try again, and eventually succeed through perseverance. Kids, just like adults, may need someone to listen carefully to their ideas and explanations. Communicating their thoughts adds to their understanding and may open up new avenues of thought. It is crucial for you to offer guidance, not answers.

It is often difficult to realize that, unlike many skills in the Content areas, problem solving is not nice and neat—it is not an "If you do these steps, you will always get this" type of thinking. Problem solving is messy. A good problem solver will try one thing, and if that fails, try another. This requires different thinking from that needed when adding three-digit numbers, which merely requires you to do the same process every time. A true problem solver starts by brainstorming many ideas and solutions, trying out the best ones until a solution (or several solutions) is found.

As the title of this section suggests, problem solving is a process or a series of steps to get to a solution. Children need to be taught those steps so they have a pattern to follow for attacking all types of problems.

The first step is to ***understand the problem***. What is it the problem all about? Children must identify the question that needs to be answered. Next, children need to differentiate important information from the information that is unimportant or irrelevant. Occasionally, children may need to discover whether any information is missing that needs to be explored before they can solve the problem. Children have to be taught to break a problem down into smaller parts, understanding each part before going on to the next. If children can put the problem in their own words, then understanding is taking place.

The second step is to **decide on a strategy** that will help find a solution to the problem. For some problems, there may be more than one strategy that will work. Likewise, children may need to employ several strategies for one problem. While certain strategies may work well with certain types of problems, different children may need to use different strategies, just because that is what works for them.

The third step is to **use the strategy to solve the problem**. Children should work the problem using the strategy they chose, recording any work. It is important for children to write down what they do so that they can see where they have been and what is still left to do. Sometimes children may find that the strategy they chose does not seem to be heading toward a solution. This is the time to try a different strategy. The goal is to find a solution; children should use whatever works.

The fourth step is to **check back**. When children find a solution for the problem, they should read the problem again to be sure that the solution fits all the conditions of the problem. It should answer the question posed. The solution should be reasonable and logical.

There are several strategies that you can teach to facilitate finding workable solutions. You may already use many of them, but were unaware that they could be taught to youngsters. The following are 10 of the most common strategies used in problem solving.

Drawing Diagrams or Pictures

Children often have difficulty visualizing problems. They may need to begin all problems by making a simple picture of what the problem is about. They may also need other strategies to solve the problem, but the first step is to understand what the problem is about. Pictures help. Making simple drawings with appropriate labels will suffice. It is a problem-solving tool, not an art project. For some problems, drawings are all that kids need to help find the solution.

Grades Pre-Kindergarten to 2

Amanda is going to the school library from her first grade class. There are eight classrooms between hers and the library. She leaves her classroom and walks down six rooms. Oops! She realizes she does not have her library books. Amanda turns around and goes back two rooms. She finds her

Amanda's Room	1	2	3	4	5	6	7	8	Library
				4	5	←			
			→		5	6	7	8	

books there, where she must have dropped them. Once again, Amanda turns around and heads for the library, counting four more classroom doors. Where is she now?

Solution: Amanda is at Room 8, next door to the library.

Grades 3 to 5

Bob runs around his block each evening after school. If the block is 280 feet long on each side, how far does Bob run?

280 feet

280 feet

Solution: 280 feet × 4 = 1,120 feet

Making a Model Using Objects

For some types of problems, children not only need to visualize what is going on, but they may also need concrete objects that they can move around. These objects can vary from actual objects that are mentioned in the problem to slips of paper with the names of the problem's objects written on them. This strategy is particularly good to use when trying to visualize relationships between objects, so that children can find a solution.

Grades Pre-Kindergarten to 2

For this problem, you will need paper, crayons, and scissors.

Four cats line up for mittens: a white cat, a yellow cat, a brown cat, and black cat. The white cat is first in line. The black cat is in front of the yellow cat. The brown cat is in front of the black cat. What color is the last cat in line?

Your child will need to color and cut out each type of cat. Your child will then have objects he or she can move around so that he or she can find the solution.

Solution: The yellow cat is last.

Grades 3 to 5

Terry is putting her stuffed animals on her three bookshelves. The shelves are stacked one on top of the other. Terry wants to arrange her animals so that there are two of them on each shelf. Her stuffed animals are Cali Cat, Dickens Dog, Harriet Hen, Marty Mouse, Penelope Pig, and Rusty Rabbit. Terry is placing Marty next to Penelope and above Rusty. She is not putting Dickens next to Penelope or Rusty. She is also not placing Cali next to Dickens. Where will Terry put each of her stuffed animals?

Your child can either use stuffed animals or write the names of each animal in the problem on cards or pieces of paper so that he or she can rearrange them to find the solution.

Solution:
Top shelf: Dickens Dog, Harriet Hen.
Middle shelf: Marty Mouse, Penelope Pig.
Bottom shelf: Rusty Rabbit, Cali Cat.

Role-Playing

Another way for children to develop understanding is to act out what is going on in the problem. When children role-play, it helps them identify with the problem and motivates them to try to solve it. Acting out a situation helps make the problem real for them.

Grades Pre-Kindergarten to 2

For this problem, you will need to have a tiled floor to use as a grid, and grid paper and a pencil for recording the solution.

Matthew is following a map to his friend's house. He walks six blocks north, turns right and walks five blocks, then turns left and walks four more blocks. Matthew arrives at his friend's house. Can you show the path he walked?

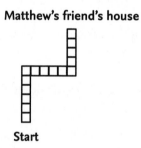

Matthew's friend's house

Start

Have your child follow the directions to walk the path on the tile floor, using one tile for each block in the problem. Then, he or she can trace the same pattern on the grid paper.

Grades 3 to 5

To act this problem out, your child will play the role of Janet and use play money (or the real thing). Someone needs to play the cashier. Your child will need to figure out the cost and the change, using the play money as an aid.

Janet went to the toy store with the $10 she received from her grandpa for her birthday. After looking at many toys, she decided to buy a puzzle for $3.50 and a stuffed bear for $5.25. How much money does Janet have left?

Solution: $1.25

Looking for a Pattern

As stated in the Content chapter on Algebra, Chapter 2, students who can recognize and use patterns have a much better understanding of mathematics than those who cannot. Identifying patterns involves organizing information and looking for relationships. Children can find patterns in sequences of actual objects, numerals, or pictures. Students need to be able to find the missing object, numeral, or picture in a sequence and then check to see if the pattern continues as predicted. If children can determine a rule for the sequence, then they can find any missing part to the sequence.

Another type of problem may require the problem solver to extend the pattern in order to find the answer. Constructing a number table allows patterns to become visible and makes the extension easy.

Grades Pre-Kindergarten to 2

Carla and her grandmother make candles for four days. They are making them as gifts to give to relatives on next week's holiday. On Monday, they make one candle. On Tuesday, they make three candles. On Wednesday, they make five candles, and on Thursday, they make seven candles. If Carla and her grandmother continue with the same pattern, how many candles will they make on Friday?

Solution: Carla and her grandmother will make nine candles on Friday.

Monday:	✕
Tuesday:	✕ ✕ ✕
Wednesday:	✕ ✕ ✕ ✕ ✕
Thursday:	✕ ✕ ✕ ✕ ✕ ✕ ✕
Friday:	?

To find the rule for a sequence of numerals, have your child look at the numbers that are given. Instruct your child to compare a number to the one that comes before it and see how it was changed to result in the number that follows it. Is it larger or smaller, and by how much? If it is larger, is something being added or multiplied to the first number to get to the following number? If it is smaller, is something being subtracted from the number, or is it being divided? How much is being added, subtracted, multiplied, or divided to the first number to get the second number in the sequence? Does this hold true for the third number in the sequence? If so, your child may have discovered the rule. In the example 1, 5, 9, 13, the rule is adding four each time. Some patterns are more complicated, such as 8, 5, 10, 7, 14, 11, 22. Here, the rule is to subtract 3 from the first number, then multiply the resulting number by 2. The next numbers would be 19, 38, 35, and so on.

Grades 3 to 5
Finish the sequences:

1, 2, 4, 8, ___, ___   **Solution:** 16, 32 (doubling)

1, 4, 9, 16, ___, ___   **Solution:** 25, 36 (square numbers)

●, ■, ●, ■, ___, ___   **Solution:** ●, ■,

ZY, YZ, YX, XY, XW, ___, ___   **Solution:** WX, WV

Making an Organized List

Problem solvers need to organize their thinking about a problem. Lists that follow some form of organization help the problem solver quickly review what has been done and figure what still needs to be finished. By having the list organized, it is easy to tell when all the possible solutions have been discovered. Note the two lists below. The Organized List lets the solver know he or she has found all the combinations.

Grades Pre-Kindergarten to 2

Austin is getting dressed for school. He has to decide what to wear. Austin has a blue shirt and a red shirt. He has a pair of white pants and a pair of black pants. What are four different sets of clothes that Austin can wear to school?

Solution:
Blue shirt and white pants.
Blue shirt and black pants.
Red shirt and white pants.
Red shirt and black pants.

Grades 3 to 5

Jenny and her friends are planning their Saturday afternoon activity. They can go to the park, the recreation center, or the school playground. They can play soccer, basketball, or baseball. To get there, they can roller blade, ride their bikes, or walk. What are all the possible combinations of activities for Jenny and her friends?

While the example at right is only a partial list of the total combinations, it is easy to see that all the possibilities involving the park are in the Organized List. It is much more difficult for the problem solver to find the solution using the strategy of the Random List.

Solution: There are 27 different combinations: nine for the park, nine for the recreation center, and nine for the playground.

RANDOM LIST

Place	Sport	Transportation
Park	Soccer	Roller blade
Rec Center	Basketball	Bike
Playground	Baseball	Walk
Rec Center	Soccer	Roller blade
Park	Baseball	Bike
Playground	Baseball	Bike
Playground	Soccer	Walk
Park	Basketball	Roller blade
Park	Basketball	Bike

ORGANIZED LIST

Place	Sport	Transportation
Park	Soccer	Roller blade
Park	Soccer	Bike
Park	Soccer	Walk
Park	Basketball	Roller blade
Park	Basketball	Bike
Park	Basketball	Walk
Park	Baseball	Roller blade
Park	Baseball	Bike
Park	Baseball	Walk

Making a Chart or Table

Tables and charts are organizational tools for problem solvers. They provide a place to arrange data so that it is easy to see all the information at a glance. Tables can also help the solver to find data that is missing or identify information that the problem asks for. Tables make patterns apparent. Today's schools often use this strategy in conjunction with other problem-solving strategies.

Grades Pre-Kindergarten to 2

Sally and Sam Squirrel are having a snack. They are eating soda crackers. Sam eats faster than Sally. In the time that Sally eats one cracker, Sam eats three crackers. The squirrels keep eating until all the crackers are gone. Sally has eaten four crackers. How many crackers has Sam eaten?

Solution: Sam will eat 12 crackers by the time Sally eats 4.

	1	2	3	4
Number of Crackers Sally Eats:	×	× ×	× × ×	× × × ×
Number of Crackers Sam Eats:	× × ×	× × × × × ×	?	?

Grades 3 to 5

Sarah and Sandy are sisters. Sarah is 5 years old and Sandy is 14 years old. When will Sandy be twice as old as Sarah?

Solution: Sandy will be twice as old as Sarah when Sarah is 9 and Sandy is 18.

Sarah	5	6	7	8	9
Sandy	14	15	16	17	18

Guess and Check

This strategy is sometimes called trial and error. For some problems, the best solution for children is to make a guess as to the possible solution and then check to see if their guess is correct. Their guess may be close to the right answer if they take time to study the problem—discarding impossible answers and using what they may already know about a similar situation. Once they check the initial guess, they repeat the procedure, narrowing down the possibilities until they discover a correct solution.

Grades Pre-Kindergarten to 2

Jerome is looking at the candy in Clara's Candy Shoppe. There are orange slices, peppermint pieces, lemon drops, cinnamon swirls, and butterscotch bits.

Jerome buys three different pieces of candy. He pays 12 cents for all of his candy. What three pieces of candy does Jerome buy?

Orange Slices
3 cents

Peppermint Pieces
4 cents

Lemon Drops
8 cents

Cinnamon Swirls
9 cents

Butterscotch Bits
1 cent

Solution:

1st guess: Orange Slice, Peppermint Piece, Lemon Drop
         3 + 4 + 8 = 15 cents (No)

2nd guess: Orange Slice, Peppermint Piece, Butterscotch Bit
         3 + 4 + 1 = 8 cents (No)

3rd guess: Orange Slice, Lemon Drop, Butterscotch Bit
         3 + 8 + 1 = 12 cents (Yes)

Jerome buys an Orange Slice, a Lemon Drop, and a Butterscotch Bit.

Grades 3 to 5

Using the numerals 1 to 8, have your child place one numeral in each box in the following figure. Numerals that are consecutive cannot be next to each other horizontally, vertically, or diagonally. For instance, 5 cannot touch 4, 7 cannot touch 8, and so on.

Solution: The numbers can also be flipped from side to side, making a mirror image resulting in this solution:

3	5		
7	1	8	2
4	6		

		5	3
2	8	1	7
		6	4

Or the solution can be flipped top to bottom, resulting in these solutions:

4	6		
7	1	8	2
3	5		

		6	4
2	8	1	7
		5	3

Another type of Guess and Check problem might be in the form of a story problem:

Bob loves cookies! He went past the bakery in the mall and saw that chocolate chip cookies were 50 cents each and sugar cookies were 35 cents each. He bought a dozen cookies for $4.65. How many of the cookies were chocolate chip?

Using Logic

As you may suspect, logic is used in all problem solving. Logical reasoning involves using higher-level thought processes. Recalling facts is simply not enough. To use logical reasoning, problem solvers must look at all the conditions in the problem and then use deductive reasoning. Some types of problems requiring logic are those that use conditional statements such as, "If this is true, then . . ."

Grades Pre-Kindergarten to 2

Dakota is playing Twenty Questions with his friends. He is thinking of an animal. Here are the clues that his friends have discovered:

> *It has four legs*
> *It has whiskers.*
> *It has a short tail.*
> *It eats carrots.*
> *It hops.*

Can you guess what animal Dakota is thinking of?

Solution: Dakota is thinking of a rabbit.

Grades 3 to 5

Here are two types of problem requiring logical reasoning:

NUMBER RIDDLE

It is a square number.
It is less than 100.
The number is not a multiple of 5.
The number is not divisible by 2.
The sum of its digits equals 13.
What is the number?

Solution:

Square numbers less than 100:	4	9	16	25	36	49	64	81
Multiple of 5:				×				
Divisible by 2:	×		×		×		×	
Digits do not equal 13:	×	×	×	×	×		×	×

The number is 49.

PLANTING A GARDEN

There are five kinds of vegetables grown in this garden: tomatoes, radishes, turnips, carrots, and squash. Each row has only one type of vegetable. The radishes and the tomatoes are red. The carrots and the squash are yellow and the turnips are white.

Using these clues, see if you can discover which vegetable is growing in each of the five rows:

	Tomatoes	Radishes	Turnips	Carrots	Squash
Row 1					
Row 2					
Row 3					
Row 4					
Row 5					

1. *The edible part of the plant in the first row does not grow underground.*
2. *In the second row, the part of the plant that is eaten is not red, but it grows underground.*
3. *The third row has a vegetable that grows underground, but it is not white.*
4. *The plant in the fourth row does not have yellow or white vegetables.*
5. *In the fifth row, the part that is eaten is not grown underground, nor is it red.*

This type of problem relies on logic and the "if, then" thought processes. Your child can use the grid to keep track of the clues. He or she can put Xs in the boxes to show what vegetable cannot be in each row. After working through all the clues and recording them on the grid, he or she can discover the answer.

Solution:
Row 1: Tomatoes
Row 2: Turnips
Row 3: Carrots
Row 4: Radishes
Row 5: Squash

Working Backward

Certain types of problems can only be solved by starting at the end. Children can do computations with the data that they find at the end of the problem. Then, the problem solver can work back through the problem, until data at the beginning of the problem can be utilized.

Grades Pre-Kindergarten to 2

Molly, Holly, and Pauly are at the school carnival. They are playing games and winning tickets that can later be used for prizes. Pauly has won the most tickets. He has three more tickets than Holly. Holly has four more tickets than Molly. Molly has only three tickets. How many tickets does Pauly have?

Solution:

Molly: 3 tickets

Holly: 3 + 4 = 7 tickets

Pauly: 7 + 3 = 10 tickets

Grades 3 to 5

Collin buys some CDs on sale. He keeps half for himself. He gives the rest to his three best friends. Each friend gets two CDs. How many CDs did Collin buy?

Solution:

2 CDs × 3 friends = 6 CDs

½ of the total CDs for himself = 6 CDs

Total = 12 CDs

Paige is looking at books in the bookstore, trying to decide which one to buy. She looks at three more adventure books than books of poetry. She looks at one half as many poetry books as fantasy books. There are one-third as many fantasy books as mysteries. She takes a long time looking at the 24 mysteries that the store is selling. How many books does she look at all together?

Solution:

Number of mysteries = 24

Fantasies (⅓ of 24) = 8

Poetry (½ of 8) = 4

Adventure (4 + 3) = 7

Total 24 + 8 + 4 + 7 = 43 books

Simplifying the Problem

With some problems, changing a difficult problem into an easier version makes it possible to figure out how to solve it. Using smaller numbers for larger ones is one way to simplify.

Grades Pre-Kindergarten to 2

In school, a teacher is telling the students about how all plants and animals depend on one another. She wants to show how a food web works. She asks Kristi, Ken, Karen, and Keith to help. Each student is connected to every other student by a piece of yarn. How many pieces of yarn are needed?

Solution:
Two Kids in the Food Web = 1 Piece of Yarn
Three Kids in the Food Web = 3 Pieces of Yarn
Four Kids in the Food Web = 6 Pieces of Yarn

Grades 3 to 5

A grocery store has 329 cans of long spear asparagus, which sell for $1.59 each, and 223 cans of cut asparagus, which sell for $1.19 each. What is the total worth of the canned asparagus?

To make the problem easier, have your child substitute smaller, rounded numbers. For example, your child should use only the closest hundred cans and the closest dollar amount: use three cans (for 300) of spear asparagus at $2.00/can, equaling $6.00, and use two cans (for 200) of cut asparagus at $1.00/can, equaling $2.00. When your child figures the value of each type, he or she can add the two types together, equaling $8.00, then multiply them by 100 to get an estimate: $800.

Now that your child has discovered the steps of multiplying the number of each type by its price and adding the two together, he or she can apply the same steps to the original problem.

Solution:
329 × $1.59 = $523.11
223 × $1.19 = $265.37
Total = $788.48

Content Connection

Problem solving is a lifelong skill that begins in infancy and is used into old age. It teaches children how to deal with problems. The important aspects are the steps, strategies, and attitudes that are being developed toward that end. At this stage, the "perfect" solution should take a back seat to learning how to be a problem solver.

The following are activities and projects from the Content Standard chapters that show how problem solving is used along with mathematical skills.

Grades Pre-Kindergarten to 2

Numbers and Operations

Exploring Measuring Cups, page 9, allows your child to use the Guess and Check strategy.

Close to the Goal, page 13, allows your child to apply the Using Logic strategy.

Algebra

Let's Clap a Rhythm, page 39, allows your child to use the Looking for a Pattern strategy.

Picture Story Problems, page 42, allows your child to use the Making a Model Using Objects strategy.

Does Everything Change? page 45, allows your child to use the Making a Chart or a Table strategy.

Geometry
Wind Sock, page 58, allows your child to use the Making a Model Using Objects strategy.

Stretch a Shape, page 60, allows your child to use the Role-Playing strategy.

Measurement
Gummy Worm Measurement, page 99, allows your child to use the Making a Model Using Objects strategy.

Estimation and Capacity, page 108, allows your child to use the Guess and Check strategy.

Data Analysis and Probability
Floor Graph, page 132, allows your child to utilize the Making a Model Using Objects strategy.

Grades 3 to 5

Numbers and Operations
What's My Number? page 18, and Number Stumpers, page 19, both allow your child to employ the Guess and Check and Using Logic strategies.

Picture This! page 22, allows your child to use the Drawing Diagrams or Pictures strategy.

Algebra
Hundreds Board Patterns, page 47, allows your child to use the Looking for a Pattern strategy.

Equation Race, page 50, allows your child to use the Working Backward strategy.

Geometry
Making a Tangram Puzzle, page 76, allows your child to utilize several strategies, including Looking for a Pattern, Using Logic, Guess and Check, and Drawing Diagrams or Pictures.

Neighborhood Map, page 83, allows your child to use the Drawing Diagrams or Pictures strategy.

Pentomino Puzzles, page 86, allows your child to utilize the Making a Model Using Objects strategy.

Measurement
Area Estimation Scramble, page 118, allows your child to employ the Using Logic strategy.

Larger than a Blue Whale? page 123, allows your child to employ both the Role-Playing and Drawing Diagrams or Pictures strategies.

Data Analysis and Probability

Who Loves Pizza? page 139, allows your child to employ both the Making an Organized List and Making a Chart or Table strategies.

Crossing the River, page 150, allows your child to apply the Using Logic strategy.

Literature Connection

Grades Pre-Kindergarten to 2

Alexander, Who Used to Be Rich Last Sunday by Judith Viorst

Caps for Sale by Esphyr Slobodkina

The Case of the Shrunken Allowance by Joanne Rocklin

Tic-Tac-Toe Three in a Row by Judith Bauer Stamper

Grades 3 to 5

Amazing Math Puzzles by Adam Hart-Davis

The Book of Think: Or How to Solve a Problem Twice Your Size by Marilyn Burns

Cool Math by Christy Maganzini

How Much Is That Guinea Pig in the Window? by Joanne Rocklin

Math Curse by Jon Scieszka

Tricky Mind Trap Puzzles by Detective Shadow

Unlock the Secrets of Your Mind by Ian Howarth and Patrick Green

Reasoning and Proof

Adults use mathematics daily: math is tool that helps us reason, sort out, and solve everyday problems. We apply those math skills we learned so long ago to help us prove our logical thinking. An example might be the desire to purchase a new car. Our reasoning may tell us that we can afford the payments or can spare to take the money from our savings accounts, but until we do the math to prove that the budget can withstand the purchase, we probably would not buy it. Being grown-ups, we do not think about this formally as "reasoning and proof," but that is basically the process we employ.

Children need to be taught that reasoning and proof are essential to being successful in mathematics. To teach this standard, today's schools instruct students of elementary age in four main objectives.

> **Children should be aware that reasoning and proof are essential parts of mathematics.**

As shown throughout the Content chapters, mathematics has little use if it is only used to add, subtract, multiply, and divide. In the "real world," these four operations are always coupled with a problem to solve and the ability to reason out the solution. Reasoning and proof are found throughout Algebra, Geometry, Measurement, Data Analysis, and as mentioned, Problem Solving.

> **Elementary students should learn to make and explore mathematical hypotheses or conjectures.**

An example of making a mathematical conjecture might be illustrated by a fourth grade class' exploration of finding the area of rectangles. After drawing various rectangles on grid paper and marking the dimensions, one student may realize that a 6-by-5-centimeter rectangle has an area of 30 square centimeters because there are 30 squares inside the rectangle. With further exploration, another child may make the conjecture that if the two dimensions (6 and 5) are multiplied, the area is also 30 square centimeters. The teacher did not tell the students the formula of A = L × W for finding the area of a rectangle. The children discovered the formula through exploration and felt free to make a conjecture.

> After they have made a conjecture, children in kindergarten to grade 5 should learn to develop and evaluate mathematical arguments and proofs concerning that conjecture.

Using the previous example, students would set out to prove that multiplying the dimensions of any rectangle would result in the same area as counting squares inside the rectangle. Further exploration might expand to whether the formula works for triangles or parallelograms. In this fashion, children evaluate conjecture and find proof.

> As children progress through the elementary school years, they should learn to select and use various types of reasoning and methods of proof.

In the early years, children base all reasoning on their perception of the world—"What you see is what you get." As they mature and progress through the elementary years, children's reasoning ability moves from the concrete to much more abstract types of reasoning. They are able to make generalizations about the relationships in mathematics, such as, "No matter which way a rectangle is cut in half (diagonally, vertically, or horizontally), all the halves have the same area."

Grades Pre-Kindergarten to 2
Young children begin using logical reasoning long before they enter school. Their reasoning ability is only limited by their narrow knowledge of the world. As their knowledge is increased by more and wider experiences, their potential for more logical reasoning also grows.

Parents can greatly affect that growth in reasoning, not only by exposing their offspring to varied experiences, but also by providing a climate that encourages and respects children in their belief that the world is supposed to make sense. Small children have their own ways of investigating mathematical occurrences and proving that their answers are true. From an adult perspective, these may seem illogical. However, if parents ask children to explain why they think something is true, it is almost always based on good reasoning ability. For the facts that they have at their disposal, the logic makes sense. It only seems like faulty reasoning to us because we have more facts with which to work.

Young students are only beginning to develop strategies to help themselves with mathematical reasoning. However, there are two strands of reasoning that today's schools teach in the early grades: recognizing patterns and classifying objects. As discussed in previous chapters, these skills help children make sense of their environment.

Young children make suppositions about the world, coming to conclusions that make sense to them and are justifiable from their limited level of experience. Giving reasons for what they think is an important skill and is a prerequisite for doing more formalized reasoning. It is important that we, as adults, do not stifle children's natural desire to think logically, just because we know more. Grown-ups have to be very careful to lend credence to youngsters' thinking.

While it is permissible to point out new facts for children to consider, a flat out, "That's wrong" can be damaging. Too much criticism can cause children to give up on trying to make conjectures and justify their thinking. It becomes a whole lot safer, from a child's perspective, not to try. Children learn to reason and use logical thinking by being encouraged to make conjectures and being allowed to prove or disprove them. This occurs if they are made to feel that their thinking, even if not justifiable from an adult level, is respected. Children need to feel secure in making conjectures and then be led to find whether they are correct or incorrect, rather than simply being told they are wrong.

Perception, or that which is seen, is the first tool that young children use in explaining their conjectures. To a kindergarten or first grade student, six pennies spread out on a table may appear as more than eight pennies in a stack. They will then need to try empirical approaches to reasoning, such as matching one penny from the table to one penny in the stack to find out which group has more. Then, they will try more abstract approaches, such as counting—for example, "There are six pennies on the table and eight pennies in the stack, so the stack has more."

By the end of second grade, students should have learned the skill of making generalizations and then testing them by finding examples. An example of a mathematical generalization at this age might be that rectangles are made up of two long sides and two short sides. Having children locate or draw many different types of rectangles helps them to explore a generalization to see if it remains true. Not only should they explore rectangles that fit the rule, but children also should be encouraged to find examples that disprove the generalization—a concept that is not easy for younger ones.

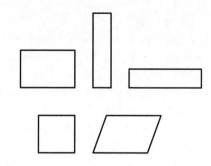

For example, these first three shapes do follow the generalization. However, the fourth is a rectangle with equal sides (commonly called a square). The fifth shape has two long sides and two short sides, but is a parallelogram instead of a rectangle.

Children should be encouraged to communicate the chains of reasoning that they develop. For instance, suppose children are trying to discover which number does not belong with the others in the sequence 7, 12, and 15. One child might say the 7, another could say the 15, and a third might say the 12. If each child communicates his or her reasoning, all three could be correct answers: 7 is the only one-digit number; 15 is the only number you say when counting by fives; and 12 is the only even number. Not only does relating their reasoning process help you as an adult to understand how they came up with a particular answer, but it also helps children reason more clearly. You can help the communication process by using mathematical vocabulary with children and encouraging them to use it when describing their mathematical ideas to you.

Some basic logic words include *not, and, or, all, some, if* _____ *then* _____, and *because*. Making sure that children understand how these words can change the meaning of a statement will help them to be able to express their chain of reasoning with more accuracy. For example, note how these sentences change just by using one of the basic logic words:

"I like oranges, not apples."
"I like oranges and apples."
"I like oranges or apples."
"I like all oranges and some apples."
"If you like oranges, then you like apples."

As a parent, you may not want to drill or turn reasoning and proof into a practice session. Enjoy the richness of children's minds by asking questions that prompt them to make conjectures about the world around them, building on their experience level. Some may be mathematical and some may not, but since reasoning permeates logical thinking in all subjects and areas of day-to-day life, everyday discussions can build this process skill.

Grades 3 to 5

By the time children reach the upper grades, making conjectures and evaluating them on the basis of evidence and proof should be common. Children should know that discovering the truth takes more than just finding a few examples that agree with their hypothesis. They should also look for any examples that disagree or disprove their arguments. Finding a range of examples allows them to make generalizations and discover relationships.

Children in grades 3 through 5 develop their reasoning about mathematical relationships. They may do this by investigating the structure of patterns. Analyzing how classes of shapes are alike and different also strengthens their reasoning ability. Children utilize mathematical reasoning when they explore the overall shape of data in graphic displays.

In the lower grades, students look at individual mathematical objects—for example, a certain number or rectangle. By the upper grades, students begin thinking about sets or classes of objects—for example, all numbers that are prime or all rectangles.

Mathematical reasoning develops in an atmosphere in which children are encouraged to express their thinking and ideas so that others can take a look. As with younger children, upper grade children must feel safe that their ideas will be valued (whether right or wrong) and not ridiculed or disrespected. You can always say, "That's an interesting idea," or, "I like how you thought about this." If the idea is on an erroneous path, you can lead the child to look further through comments such as, "Have you thought about . . . ?" or, "Do you think there could be other possibilities?" Part of learning to reason mathematically is examining and understanding why something appears to be true, but is not. Often a "wrong" idea creates an opportunity for discussion and new discoveries in mathematics. Not always being "right" is part of the journey in reasoning and logic. Once again, it is a case of guiding thinking, not imposing adult knowledge.

Often the very process of children explaining their thinking and having to justify it to someone else will set them on the correct path. Most adults experience the same thing from time to time. There seems to be something inherently self-correcting about verbalizing our thinking processes. It is easy to forget that children need to do the same thing, too.

The more children can explain their ideas—and discover their own mistakes—the better they become at spotting truth and fallacy in others' ideas. This does not happen overnight. It takes time, a variety of experiences, and supportive guidance for children to become adept at making valid arguments and being able to judge the arguments of others.

Parents can help their children become competent in mathematical reasoning by encouraging them to verbalize their ideas, both mathematical and otherwise, and to justify why they think what they think. Reasoning is learned by example as well. Children will learn by example when they hear a parent say, "This is what I think and this is why I think it is true."

Not only should children share their ideas and be listened to respectfully, but they also need to learn to listen to others' ideas and reasoning. Children have a responsibility to try to understand others' ideas as well as their own. Family discussions are invaluable for both learning to reason and for learning to listen to someone else's ideas, beliefs, and conjectures about the world.

The following are activities and projects from the Content Standard chapters that show how reasoning and proof is used along with other mathematical skills.

Grades Pre-Kindergarten to 2

Numbers and Operations
How High or Low Can You Go? page 5, allows your child to use reasoning skills while examining the place value of numbers.

Algebra
Mystery Box, page 37, helps your child develop reasoning skills by repeating this activity over time.

Geometry
Coordinate Pair Tic-Tac-Toe, page 64, allows your child to use reasoning skills to play the game—and the proof is in the winning.

Mirror Symmetry, page 67, is a good exercise for your child to prove conjectures about symmetry.

Measurement
How Long Does It Take? page 108, allows your child to practice making conjectures and proving them.

Data Analysis and Probability
Number Cube Tally, page 135, has your child practice gathering data and using reasoning skills to make conjectures with rolls of number cubes.

Grades 3 to 5

Numbers and Operations
I Want More, page 21, allows your child to use reasoning and proof in exploring fractions.

Just Ask Me, page 24, allows your child to employ reasoning skills while practicing number characteristics.

Algebra
Toothpick Tussle, page 48, has your child use reasoning to solve a patterning problem.

Geometry
Mystery Guess and Check, page 82, has your child use reasoning skills to locate his or her opponent on a hidden grid.

Measurement
Ruler of the House, page 112, has your child employ estimation as a conjecture and measurement as a proof.

Capacity Calculations, page 120, has your child utilize reasoning to develop a way to measure a balloon's capacity.

Data Analysis and Probability

Experiment Model of Data Analysis, page 138, has your child conduct an experiment using brands of bubble gum to show proof of a hypothesis.

Better or Worse, page 144, has your child evaluate different types of graphic displays using reasoning skills.

Literature Connection

Grades Pre-Kindergarten to 2

Lon Po Po by Ed Young

More for Me by Sydnie Meltzer Kleinhenz

Grades 3 to 5

The I Hate Mathematics! Book by Marilyn Burns

Math for Smarty Pants by Marilyn Burns

Right in Your Own Backyard: Nature Math by Time-Life Books

Sideways Arithmetic from Wayside School by Louis Sachar

Communication

8

Communication is basically a way to exchange ideas and thoughts with another person. This can be done by speaking, with gestures and body language, with pictures, by manipulating objects, by using symbols, or through writing. As human beings, communication is one of our most cherished needs and, at the same time, one of our most powerful tools. Without it, there would be no learning. As a parent, you use this tool daily to guide your child toward mature reasoning. It is also the basis for all educational processes, mathematics included.

The following four skills are recommended to help students communicate successfully about mathematics.

> **Students should learn to organize and consolidate their mathematical ideas, concepts, and reasoning through communication.**

When children communicate their ideas about mathematics, it helps them to organize their thinking, make their thoughts more clear, and bring their thoughts all together into a consolidated whole. The very act of communicating an idea, whether it is through speech or the written word, forces an individual to make that thought coherent. Ever wonder why people talk to themselves, even when no one is around? This is how we organize our thinking, mathematical or not.

> **Children in elementary grades should learn to communicate mathematical thinking clearly and logically to their teachers, classmates, parents, and others.**

The more children are allowed to express ideas to people of all age groups and give their reasoning for those ideas, the better they become at communicating clearly. The same is true for mathematical thinking—as it is for all areas of communication. Communication skills require practice, just like playing soccer or the piano.

> **Elementary students should begin to critically examine and weigh the mathematical thinking and strategies that others use.**

Communication is not just having someone listen to you. It is also listening carefully to what someone else says and analyzing that person's ideas. In some ways, this is a more difficult skill for children, because developmentally they are more "me"-oriented. Adults can model this behavior by showing how to listen attentively and by asking children questions about their ideas.

> **As children progress through the elementary years, they should become increasingly able to use mathematical language to express their ideas distinctly and definitely.**

Children should be encouraged by teachers and parents to use more precise language as they grow in their communication skills. While this is true in all areas of communication, it is particularly important for the development of mathematical thinking. Some mathematical ideas are difficult to explore without precise math vocabulary to define the thought.

Grades Pre-Kindergarten to 2

Mathematical communication begins early in children's lives. Before entering school, they communicate their needs by wanting more juice or a different stuffed animal at bedtime. As their number sense develops, pre-school children may ask for two cookies. The level of a child's ability to communicate mathematically is based on several factors: how mature the child is, how rich the child's exposure to mathematical language is, and how varied the child's experiences and opportunities in the world are.

We all know that language and vocabulary development is important to children's ability to learn to read. Language is equally important to children in learning mathematics. Parents along with teachers should help children talk, demonstrate, and write about mathematics. You can achieve this by having children explain how they got a particular answer—for example, "What was going on in your head to lead you to this answer?" Kids should be encouraged to tell what strategies they used.

When children communicate their steps toward solving a problem, it makes their thinking observable. It also makes what they are doing more understandable and clearer to them.

Suppose that a first grade class was trying to solve the following problem: Three bears were walking in the woods. They met seven more bears. They decided to have a picnic. How many bears were at the picnic?

One child might line up all the bears and count: 1, 2, 3, 4, 5, 6, 7, 8, 9, 10. Another child might solve the problem by taking two bears from the group of seven, making two groups of five and use the addition fact 5 + 5 (a fact they already know) to solve the problem. A third child might use counters to represent the bears, but count them by twos. Only by listening to children communicate how they got their answers do we really know what they are thinking.

Children will not find this reflection on their own thought processes easy at first. It takes time and practice. It is amazing, however, that once kids learn to explain their ideas mathematically, their mathematical knowledge seems to expand rapidly.

It is true that young students are more adept at talking and listening than they are at reading and writing. In the early years, children find moving real objects or drawing pictures an easy way to communicate. However, they also need to explore using writing and diagrams or charts to explain their answers to various math problems. It may be that their writing and diagrams will be somewhat incomprehensible to us, but it sets the stage for more formalized writing. Be prepared for some creative and unique representations of their answers. Couple children's written explanations with them telling you what they have written. Not only does this help you make sense of their attempts at written communication, but it also gives kids double practice as they speak and write about their solution to a math problem.

Likewise, when you are explaining your own ideas to children, it is important to model a variety of ways to communicate. Use pictures, manipulate objects, draw diagrams, or write simple instructions in addition to using oral communication. Mathematical communication can be a positive time for sharing. Most of all, enjoy watching your child grow and revel in that special oneness that occurs between a child and a parent with good communication of any kind.

The following are some communication practice ideas.

Daily Diaries

Make a diary out of age-appropriate lined paper and alternating pages of plain paper. Have your primary-age child write a description of his or her day, writing in the clock times telling when he or she did a particular activity. Your child can use the plain paper to draw the activity and use the lined paper to write a sentence describing the activity. At first he or she may need your assistance in writing the sentence. For very young children, simply have them make the drawing and tell you what it shows. They may dictate a sentence for you to write.

Picture Facts

As your child learns the addition and subtraction facts, have him or her write the fact at the top of a piece of paper. Then, he or she can make a picture that shows the fact. Let your child tell you the story that the picture and fact are about.

Spending Money

Have your first grade child make a chart to show how many ways there are to make 25 cents, using pictures of coins. Your child can illustrate the chart by showing different things that can be bought for that amount. You can adapt this idea to other ages by changing the amount of money. Use a dime for kindergarteners and up to a dollar for second graders.

Grades 3 to 5

As children mature, their ability to read, write, listen, think, and communicate about mathematical problems, concepts, and ideas develops and improves. Since their overall ability to read and write has grown considerably, upper elementary students communicate in both written and oral form in a much clearer and more focused manner than they did when they were in the primary grades.

As with younger students, upper grade children also need to be encouraged to use math vocabulary when they are communicating about math problems. If they are writing about math, these older students should be expected to communicate coherently using complete sentences and complete thoughts to express their ideas. After all, students would do this if they were working on a reading or language project. Clear communication is equally important in math.

Children of this age group are becoming less "me"-oriented and more concerned with their peers. Therefore, they are also much more adept at learning and working with others. In school, students in third through fifth grade often take part in group discussions in order to understand, question, and evaluate conjectures. Brainstorming often takes place to expand upon an idea put forth by someone in the group. Working in these groups gives students a chance to be both the one communicating thoughts and also the one listening, analyzing, and evaluating another individual's mathematical thinking.

As children mature, when they ask questions about something that is not clear, it is a sign that they are taking responsibility for their own learning. This is an ideal time to open up the communication lines between parent and child. A question is an opportunity to make models of a problem or to draw a picture or diagram. Children need to be led to recognize that the focus is not on who is right and who is wrong, but rather on whether or not an answer makes sense and is reasonable. In a relaxed and supportive atmosphere, children will regard not knowing something as a positive opportunity to explore and communicate. All questions are good questions, providing a wonderful opportunity for a family to share a discovery together!

Here are some communication practice ideas for the upper grade child.

Communicating About Math Games

Have your child write a letter to grandparents (or an aunt, uncle, or cousin) telling the steps needed to play a math game.

Have your child teach a math game to a younger sibling or to a friend.

Communicating Directions

Ask your child to write directions in complete sentences from your home to a friend's house. Tell him or her to pretend it is for a new student in school who has never been to the friend's house before.

Have your child make a diagram of the set of directions from your home to the friend's house.

Vacation Math

When taking a family trip, have your upper grade child keep a family log of the vacation. The log can include such things as how long it took to get from one destination to another. Your child can keep track of the cost of fuel, food, and lodging in a chart. Your child can also keep a list of the numbers he or she saw while traveling, or can turn this into a game to see who finds the most. At the end of the day, your child could write a descriptive summary of the day's activities, including some of the information found in the charts and list.

Television Math

While watching television, have your child take notes about the mathematical things he or she sees. Then, your child can write a word problem about the information that he or she has seen.

World Records

Kids love the *Guinness Book of World Records*. It is published yearly and is found in most libraries. Your child can make a list of his or her favorite facts and records, including the record-breaking numbers found in them. Using his or her own words, let your child write about the most amazing records.

Caveman Math

To help a child learn to communicate clearly and coherently, it is fun to challenge him or her to explain a math concept to a caveman (or an alien)—someone who has no prior knowledge of our mathematical system. At first, it is a struggle, but if done often, your child will get more precise in using communication skills.

For instance, have your child explain a rectangle to the caveman:

"It has four sides," your child may say.

"Like this?" you might say and draw any four-sided figure.

"No, the sides that are across from each other go the same way," your child responds.

"Like this?" you say.

"No, it's not all squished like that. It has corners like a box," he or she says.

"Like this?" you may ask.

"Yes, that is it."

"So, a rectangle has four sides with its opposite sides parallel and it has four right angle corners."

As a parent, you need to play at being an ignorant caveman or lost alien and draw something that fits the child's description, but does not fit what has *not* been said. Kids will often think this is funny as they struggle to make the "caveman" understand.

As your child practices Caveman Math, he or she will learn to incorporate mathematical vocabulary and think more precisely.

Some more ideas to explore in this activity, besides geometric shapes, are:

- Explain how you do long division (or multiplication).
- Explain regrouping in subtraction or addition.
- Explain what you need to do to measure a distance that is longer than your measuring tool.
- Explain how to add (subtract, multiply, or divide) on a calculator.
- Explain how to tell time using an analog clock.

Positive communication between parent and child is an extremely powerful tool that is not only useful for teaching those things you value, but also for building self-esteem and strong family bonds. You should help your child communicate mathematically in a relaxed atmosphere that allows for growth and for error. It should be another opportunity for family sharing and caring.

The following are some recommendations for activities involving communication that are in the Content Standard chapters.

Grades Pre-Kindergarten to 2

Numbers and Operations
Mathematical Simon Says, page 15, helps your child develop listening skills.

Algebra
Let's Clap a Rhythm, page 39, also helps your child develop listening skills.

Picture Story Problems, page 42, teaches math communication by having your child write his or her own math stories.

Geometry
Look Where You're Going, page 63, allows your child to explore communication about map directions.

Measurement
Guess What Tool to Use, page 103, is a guessing game that has your child use oral communication skills about measurement tools.

Data Analysis and Probability
Posing Questions, page 130, discusses how to teach your child to ask clear questions.

Grades 3 to 5

Numbers and Operations

Number Stumpers, page 19, has your child use written clues that lead an opponent to a selected number.

Algebra

Riddle Me This, page 51, has your child write riddles and equations about multiplication facts.

Story Problem Book, page 53, has your child write stories ending with a mathematical question.

Geometry

How's Your Book Shaping Up? page 74, has your child create a book about the properties of shapes.

Math Talk, Pure and Simple, page 79, discusses ways for you and your child to communicate about math.

How Did You Do? page 89, has your child write directions and draw diagrams for tangram designs.

Measurement

Write a Riddle, page 127, has your child write riddles using measurement data about household objects.

Data Analysis and Probability

Survey Model of Data Analysis, page 137, Research Model of Data Analysis, page 138, and Experiment Model of Data Analysis, page 138, each allow your child to utilize graphic displays to communicate results.

Connections

Knowledge of any kind is of little use if it can only be used in one narrow circumstance. Suppose we watch the weather report on television and find that the temperature will be 30 °F (–1 °C) tomorrow. That is an interesting fact that we understand, but we could not utilize that information if we did not make many connections with the fact. Those connections tell us that we need to dress warmly for the day. We may have to scrape the ice on our car's windows before going to work. The dog's water needs to be checked. It might be advisable to get a road report to see if driving could be hazardous. Making connections allows us to make sense of the world we live in.

As children grow and experience life, they, too, begin to make connections in their daily lives. At times we may find the little ones amusing when they make an assumption that is incorrect, just because they have not made all the connections that more mature individuals do. An example might be that a kindergartner would rather have a handful of ten pennies than three dimes. The child has not made the connection that coins have different values, and that he or she can purchase more with the dimes than with the pennies. The handful of ten seems like much more than merely three coins.

There are three objectives that children need to work toward in making connections in mathematics.

> **Children should identify and use connections among the different math concepts and ideas.**

Children who are able to see the relationship between mathematical ideas will find the subject much easier to understand. Realizing that addition and subtraction are not totally different things, but rather just opposite from one another, makes both comprehensible. Understanding that multiplication is simply the repeated addition of a number takes away the mystery and foreignness of learning those "times" tables.

Kindergarten through fifth grade students should comprehend how math concepts are interconnected and how one builds on another, thus allowing mathematics to make sense as a whole.

Besides seeing that some concepts are related, children need to see that if they know one concept well, the next one is connected and a part of the whole. Mathematics is not a bunch of unrelated information that is impossible to keep track of. Understanding multiplication makes figuring the area of a rectangle possible, which leads to figuring the volume of a rectangular container, and so on.

Elementary students should understand that mathematical ideas and concepts may be applied in many areas besides mathematics.

Often children only see mathematics as a school subject. They are surprised to learn that they were using mathematics at their soccer game or when they helped Dad put up a fence around the yard for the dog. Mathematics is not only a real-life skill; it is also used in many other disciplines, such as science, social studies, music, and the arts.

Grades Pre-Kindergarten to 2

One of the most important connections that children in the early grades need to make concerning mathematics is to relate the informal math that they have acquired through their everyday experiences to the math that is taught to them in school. All the other connections that children make in mathematics are based on this one foundation. In order for students to make their discoveries in math meaningful and sensible, they must rest on this all-important connection between school and home.

One in four adults say they had or still have a fear of math. At the time many grown-ups were in school, math was taught as a series of isolated topics with little or no connection among each other or among other subjects. It really didn't make sense. Teachers did not make the connections between the "real world" and school mathematics.

It is important that you as a parent do not pass on your fear to your child. Even though your experience with school mathematics might have been "scary," you can support your child's mathematical success by providing opportunities to experience math in an informal manner. The emphasis of this book has been to show how parents are invaluable in helping kids find mathematical meaning through games, projects, and activities. It is these kinds of endeavors that promote the connections that need to be made between life and school. Understanding connections breaks down the wall that so often separates school math from everyday life. It allows children to see the beauty of mathematics: it is a way to see the world more clearly and to be able to represent and understand the world they live in.

Become aware of the large role mathematics plays in everything you do day in and day out. Point out these situations to your young mathematician. Let your child know that when you are making the costume for his or her school play, you are using measurements and fractions. Discuss how you use addition and weight measurement when grocery shopping. When taking a trip by car, demonstrate how the odometer (on analog odometers) keeps track of mileage and how liquid measurement is used when buying gas. These are the meaningful, yet informal, mathematics that make later connections possible.

When helping your child at home with school mathematics, help him or her see that math topics are not isolated from one another. For instance, addition is not just a lone topic. Addition is the opposite of subtraction. It is the basis for multiplication. Adding is used when you want to put sets of objects together.

Students will better understand the relationships among the various topics of mathematics if they experience them in purposeful projects. One activity presented in the chapter on Algebra, Chapter 2, illustrates how you can easily integrate math topics into activities. Hors d'Oeuvres Are in Order (page 40) gives a meaningful opportunity to study pattern and counting, and it could include addition and subtraction—for example, "There are three pieces of fruit on the skewer. How many would there be if you put three more pieces on?" Ah, connections!

Your primary age child can explore connections by counting when he or she jumps rope or by using geometric shapes, symmetry, or patterning when creating art. Your child can sort leaves or shells when he or she goes on a nature walk, or find patterns in the songs, poetry, and stories he or she experiences when reading or when someone else is reading aloud.

The best connections in mathematics are often made when children are challenged by a lengthy project. In making or building something with Mom or Dad, they may be doing new mathematics that they have not yet encountered in school. Helping measure the boards for the new doghouse may introduce a new measurement unit or tool. While these "new" mathematics concepts may not be mastered, it will greatly enhance children's learning when the concepts are later introduced in school.

Grades 3 to 5
As children progress from third through fifth grade, they will encounter a large amount of new content in math. The degree of success they will have in understanding and utilizing this new content will be seated in how well teachers and parents connect ideas to what kids already know. These connections let students see mathematics as a whole related body of knowledge instead of the isolated topics that you may have endured as a child.

One of the major connections that teachers in the upper grades stress is equivalence. This means that students make connections among like amounts—for example, one-fourth is equivalent to 0.25, or 25 percent. Another example comes from measurement—1 quart is equivalent to 4 cups, or 2 pints, or 32 ounces. This sense of equivalence helps to bring a feeling of connectedness to mathematics, a feeling that studying fractions is not totally different from studying decimals or percentages. Building connections for mathematics through real-life projects not only strengthens math skills and understanding, but it also strengthens skills in other disciplines, such as reading, science, or social studies.

In grades 3 to 5, students begin delving into the processes needed for scientific inquiry. Scientific processes often entail using significant mathematics. When children perform experiments, they must classify (sort and look for patterns), measure, record data (use charts and tables), draw conclusions from the data, and communicate their findings. They may have to justify their results. These are all processes and skills used in mathematics.

As children mature, mathematics and other disciplines become more and more intertwined. When students see that similar mathematics is used in different disciplines and contexts, they become aware of how powerful a tool it really is. Parents can help their children notice that even though they are doing social studies or science homework, mathematics is also involved. Discovering connections between mathematics and "real-life" situations and between math and other subjects will support all learning. Mathematics can become exciting and challenging to children when it is built on a basis of connections.

The Content chapters discussed many games, activities, discussions, and projects. The following activities and projects are good ways to show how mathematics is connected within itself and with other topics.

Grades Pre-Kindergarten to 2

Numbers and Operations

Cooking, page 10, allows your child to connect real-life skills to fractions, measuring tools and units, and temperature.

Mathematical Simon Says, page 15, allows your child to connect computation skills, following directions, and careful listening.

Algebra

Hors d'Oeuvres Are in Order, page 40, allows your child to connect patterning, addition, subtraction, and family responsibility.

Does Everything Change? page 45, allows your child to connect recording data, measuring length and weight, and making predictions.

Geometry

Bedroom Map, page 62, allows your child to connect geometric shapes, visualization, directions, and location.

Neighborhood Scavenger Hunt, page 71, allows your child to connect two- and three-dimensional shapes, visualization, directions, and recording data.

Measurement

Is It Longer, Shorter, or Just the Same? page 100, allows your child to connect measurement, sorting, and data representation.

Towering Blocks, page 104, allows your child to connect measurement, estimation, recording data, and computation to keep score.

Data Analysis and Probability

Small Grid Graphing, page 134, allows your child to connect sorting, tallying, counting, recording data, analyzing data, and communication.

Grades 3 to 5

Numbers and Operations

Just Ask Me, page 24, allows your child to connect math vocabulary, logic, and a review of math concepts.

I Know What It Costs, page 26, allows your child to connect addition, subtraction, money, and real-life skills.

Algebra

Story Problem Book, page 53, allows your child to connect computation, equations, writing, reading, and formulating questions.

Weather Reporter, page 55, allows your child to connect using measurement tools for temperature and precipitation, reading weather charts and graphs, recording data, making a chart or table, analyzing data, and using negative numbers.

Geometry

Pinwheel, page 87, allows your child to connect rotational geometry, fractions (halves, fourths), math vocabulary (*diagonal, square, triangle*), following directions, science concepts, and wind force.

Quilt Block Pillow, page 92, allows your child to connect geometric shapes, measurement, patterning, visualization, following directions, and math vocabulary.

Measurement

Using Paces to Estimate, page 123, allows your child to connect measurement, estimation, multiplication, division, and calculator skills.

Building Models of Area and Volume, page 127, allows your child to connect measurement, visualization, area, volume, and geometric shapes.

Data Analysis and Probability

Best Popcorn Buy, page 140, allows your child to connect the scientific method of inquiry, collecting and recording data, logical thinking, problem solving, and communication through graphing.

Who's the Coolest? page 147, allows your child to connect reading maps, U.S. geography, collecting and recording data, using data to draw conclusions, and temperature.

Representation

In the broadest sense of the word, *representation* means anything that brings a picture to the mind—it may be an image, diagram, or drawing; it may be words that depict an idea; or it may be a message made through body language or gestures. Graphical displays and tables are other possibilities. Or a representation could be symbolic—both those invented and the more standard or accepted symbols we all recognize. How many times have you struggled to understand what someone was explaining to you and finally said, "Can you draw a picture of it?" When it was put before you in a graphic sense, it all became clear. We use representations throughout many aspects of our lives. Using representations of all types to express mathematical ideas is at the core of understanding mathematics.

There are three main objectives for elementary students in the use of representations.

> **Elementary students should develop their ability to create and use representations so that they can organize, record, and communicate mathematical ideas.**

The main reason for making representations is so that students can better understand mathematical ideas or more easily solve problems. Representations allow them to get it all out in front of them, so that they can organize their thinking and keep track of what they are doing. It also helps them communicate their solutions or conjectures to someone else.

In order to solve problems, grade school students should learn to choose, utilize, and translate from one form to another among mathematical representations.

Children need to learn which type of representation will be of the most help in solving a particular problem. Will a picture do? Do I need to build a model to understand what is going on? Would a graph make the information clearer and more easily understood? Sometimes the use of one type of representation needs to be changed to another type in order to get the clearest image. Changing a picture representation to an equation may be an advantage for some types of problems. This is translating a representation from one form to another.

Students should begin to develop their use of representations to model and understand real-life phenomena, whether they are physical, social, or mathematical.

As children become more proficient in making and using representations, this process skill, hopefully, will be transferred to many areas of everyday living. Representations are a part of real life—for example, a diagram showing how to assemble a barbecue grill or the graphs found in newspapers that show weather data or the number of households with computers. Children, too, can develop their ability to create and understand their own representations of their "real world."

Grades Pre-Kindergarten to 2
Primary students represent their thinking about mathematical problems in a variety of ways. They may draw pictures, often needing to offer an oral explanation so that you can understand what they are representing. They love to tell you what they are doing, even though their language skills in communicating precise ideas are limited. When words fail them, children in the early grades rely on physical gestures, body language, or role-playing. They begin to delve into the world of symbols, though they may be ones you have never seen. They will learn more conventional symbols as they progress through the grades.

Many of these representations are a natural result of children's need to communicate and relate to the environment in which they live. To connect this innate need to make representations of the world around them to mathematics, children simply need guidance and experience so that they can realize the full benefit of using representations to solve problems.

These representations are powerful tools for thinking as well as communicating. Not only do they help students clarify their own thinking processes, but they also allow a window into children's reasoning. This lets parents and teachers gain insight as to what is going on in the wonderful brain of a child.

Children need to be encouraged to use multiple methods to represent their ideas. A first grader who uses his or her fingers to count is using a physical representation. The child can follow this up with drawing pictures of the objects counted, counting out loud, or writing the numerals (symbols). At times, children may use representations that are not traditionally used by adults. That is completely acceptable. Their inventive representations still provide a way to record their mathematical thinking and a way to glimpse the level of understanding they have achieved.

When children make representations, it makes a mathematical problem more concrete or realistic. It also leaves a record so that children can look back and reflect upon what they have already done. Let's suppose that a student is doing a problem requiring more than one step:

Brenda is figuring how many wings there are in her insect collection. She has four bugs with two wings each and three bugs with four wings each. Brenda might make the following representation to help her organize her thinking.

Primary level children often use real objects that they can rearrange and move to represent their mathematical thinking. Brenda could have represented her insects by drawing and cutting out bugs from paper so that she could move them around and group them. In the previous example, she has invented her own symbolic bugs. The use of physical objects and invented symbols lays the groundwork for using standard math symbols in later years.

By using representations, students can easily see and understand how mathematical situations that seem quite different are in fact closely related. Take, for instance, the various ways that subtraction is used. There is the "take away" situation—for example, "There are six cookies and Bobby ate four. How many are left?" (6 − 4 = 2.) There is also the comparison situation—for example, "Sally has six books. Ted has four books. How many more does Sally have than Ted?" (Also 6 − 4 = 2.) Finally, there is the missing addend or quantity problem—for example, "Jack put four pennies in his bank. How many more pennies does he need to put in to have six pennies?" (4 + [box] = 6 or 6 − 4 = 2.) To children, these three problem types seem separate and distinct. However, if they employ a representation for each one, it becomes apparent that all three require subtraction.

Children need to be encouraged to talk about their representations. By giving voice to their work, they may be able to see other possibilities or new ways to explain their thinking. It also shows how well they understand the mathematics they are trying to represent. We know as adults that representations in the grown-up world are often open to various interpretations. Children, too, may interpret diagrams, charts, and symbols differently than you might expect. By listening as they talk about their representations, it is possible for adults to see how they are thinking.

Grades 3 to 5

Students in grades 3 to 5 continue to develop and employ a variety of representations. At this level, they use drawings, models, equations, charts, and graphs in problem solving, to explore mathematical relationships, and to justify or disprove a mathematical statement. Students are making a representation when they are showing weather data, as in the activity Who's the Coolest? (page 147). Likewise, when students translate a problem into a mathematical equation, they are using a representation. These are all tools to aid thinking and make the communication of an idea easier.

It has been found that students who use some type of representation when trying to solve a problem are more likely to see important aspects and relationships than students who do not attempt a representation. As stated in chapter 6, "Problem Solving," staring at a blank page and hoping for a solution is seldom successful. Once children put something down on that paper—pictures, symbols, equations—then their thinking has a place to begin.

While many of the basic ideas for using representations are the same as in the lower grades, in the upper elementary years students become comfortable using equations and conventional symbols. They understand that the equal sign (=) is like the balance point on a scale—what is on one side of the equal sign (or scale) has to be of the same value (or weight) as what is on the other side. The symbols < (less than) and > (greater than) are commonly used. Older students are introduced to inequalities as well (≠).

Depending upon the school system, students in grades 3 to 5 are introduced to technological tools. They may have access to a variety of mathematical software that they can utilize for representations. Students may learn to use simple spreadsheets to record data and then use that data to solve problems or look for patterns.

As with many other aspects of mathematics, various types of representation should not be taught in isolation. It may be advantageous, from time to time, to examine different types of representation so that children can consider the plusses and minuses of each type. However, a particular representation is only meaningful if it is a useful tool for children in understanding an idea or communicating information.

The following are some activities found in the Content Standard chapters that help teach your child about using representations.

Grades Pre-Kindergarten to 2

Numbers and Operations

What Does a Number Look Like? page 5, has your child use manipulatives to represent the place value of two-digit numbers.

Writing Equations, page 11, has your child use real objects to represent equations.

Algebra

Clothespin Addition and Subtraction, page 43, has your child make a model of addition and subtraction problems using clothespins.

Geometry

Frozen Geometric Solids, page 59, has your child make models of three-dimensional shapes from frozen Kool-Aid.

Magic Picture Folds, page 67, has your child make visual models showing symmetry.

Measurement

Is It Longer, Shorter, or Just the Same? page 100, has your child use a Venn diagram to show comparisons.

Families by the Yard, page 102, has your child use lengths of string to represent family members' height.

Data Analysis and Probability

What's Really in a Bag of M&M's? page 131, has your child make a bar graph using M&M's.

Floor Graph, page 132, has your child use real objects and a large floor graph to make representations.

Small Grid Graphing, page 134, has your child use 1-inch grid paper and small snack bags to make representations.

Grades 3 to 5

Numbers and Operations

Roll a Rectangular Array, page 25, has your child use grid paper to make models of multiplication facts.

Algebra

Hundreds Board Patterns, page 47, has your child use Hundreds Boards to make a visual display of multiples.

Rectangular Array, page 54, has your child use models to illustrate multiplication, division, perimeter, and area.

Geometry

Pinwheel, page 87, has your child make a pinwheel to model rotational symmetry.

Marshmallow and Toothpick Geometry, page 88, has your child make models of two- and three-dimensional shapes using marshmallows and toothpicks.

Thinking in Three Dimensions, page 90, has your child use nets to show how two-dimensional shapes become three-dimensional shapes.

Measurement

Family Metric Smile, page 111, has your child make a representation of the total length of the smiles of each family member.

Changing Perimeters and Areas, page 117, has your child use grid paper and string to figure area and the perimeter of a child's hand or foot.

Larger than a Blue Whale? page 123, has your child mark off the length of a blue whale in an outdoor area to make a representation and then note any comparisons.

Discovering Formulas, page 125, has your child use grid paper to discover the formulas for area and perimeter of geometric shapes.

Data Analysis and Probability

What Are the Odds? page 142, has your child utilize a recording sheet in which tallies represent the frequency of numbers shown on dice rolls.

Brand X or Brand Y? page 145, has your child make three different graphic displays to represent data collected on a survey sheet.

Summing It Up

Each of the Process Standards—Problem Solving, Reasoning and Proof, Communication, Connections, and Representations—has been discussed in isolation and in depth. In the real world of mathematics, people use these skills together, not individually. How can you solve a problem if you do not use reasoning? Could you understand a problem if it were not for making representations? In order to solve any problem, you need to make many mathematical connections. Also, at some point, a problem solver will want to communicate the solution to the problem to someone—a teacher, a parent, or, as an adult, a boss.

The activities in the Content Standard chapters are based on incorporating many of the Process Standards. All these standards naturally go together when solving meaningful mathematical problems, playing games, building or creating projects, and working in other subject areas in school. Teaching kids to *do* math in everyday living will allow them to learn, be successful, and actually enjoy the exciting and challenging world of mathematics.

Appendix

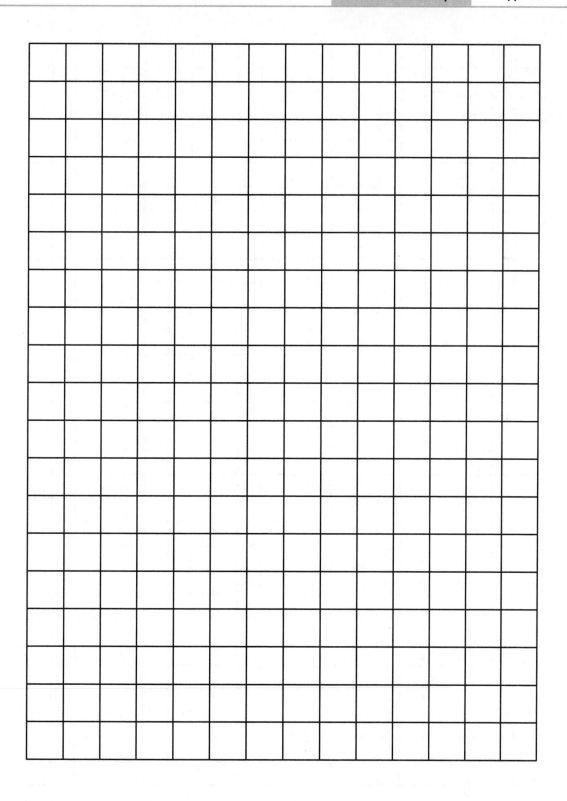

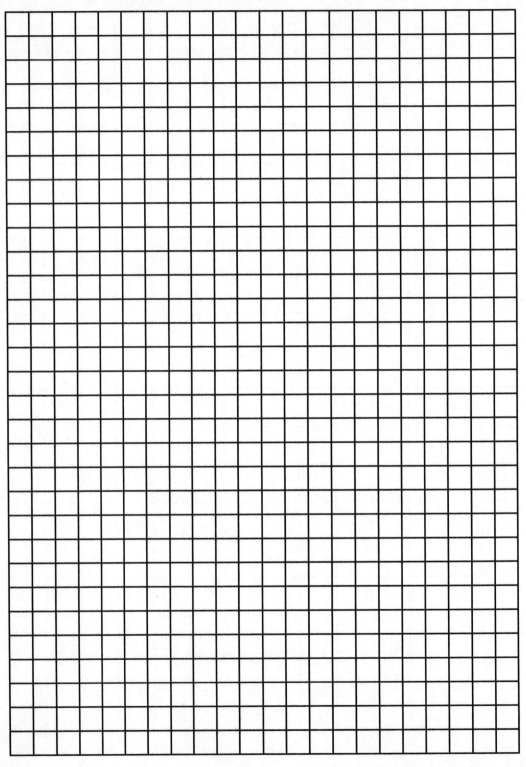

Twelfths

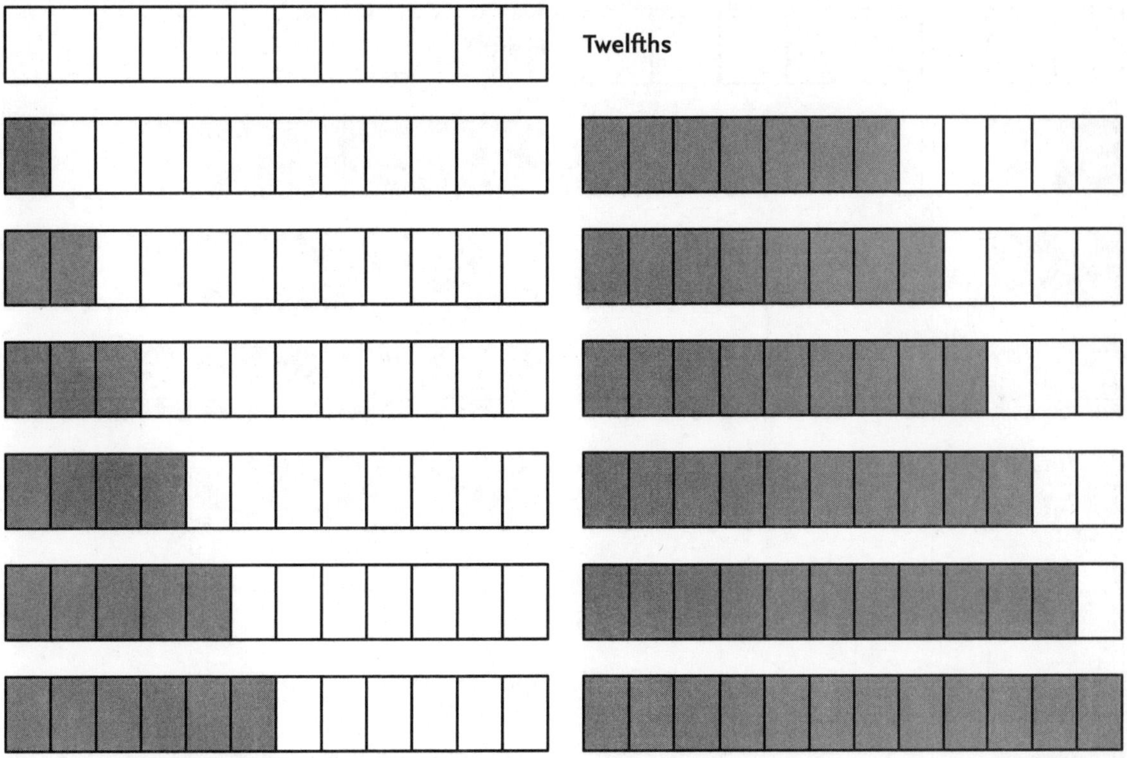

Sixths

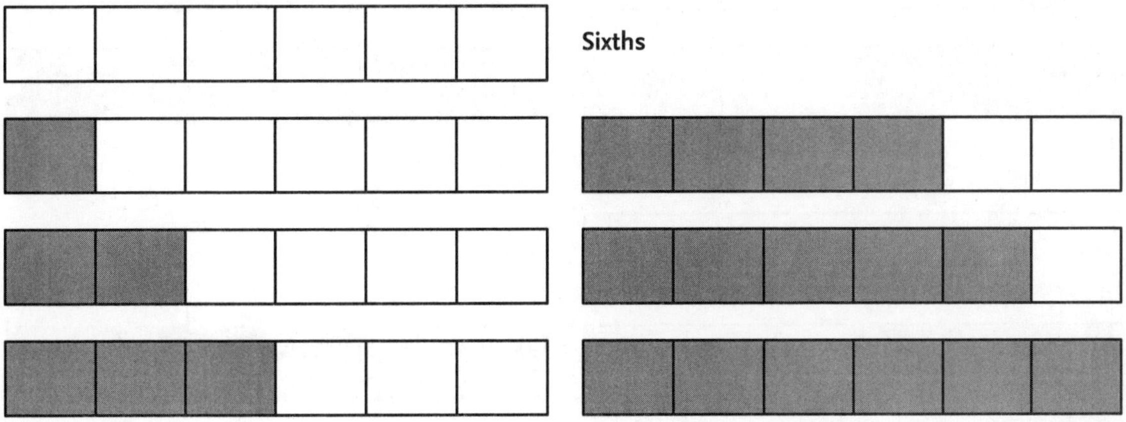

Thirds

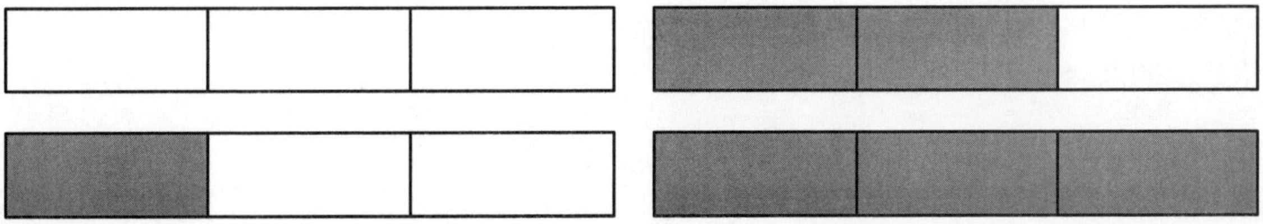

Eighths

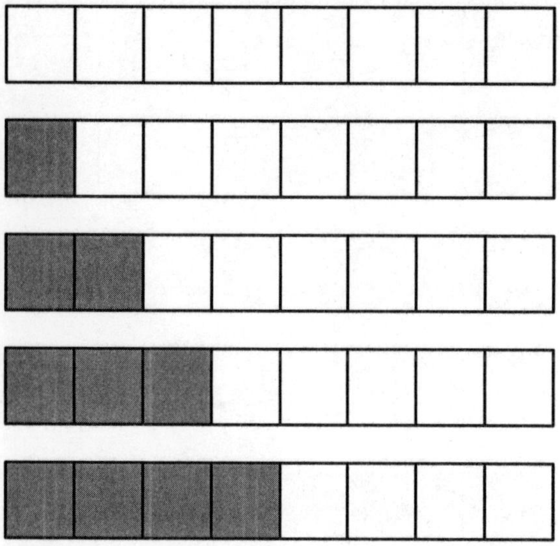

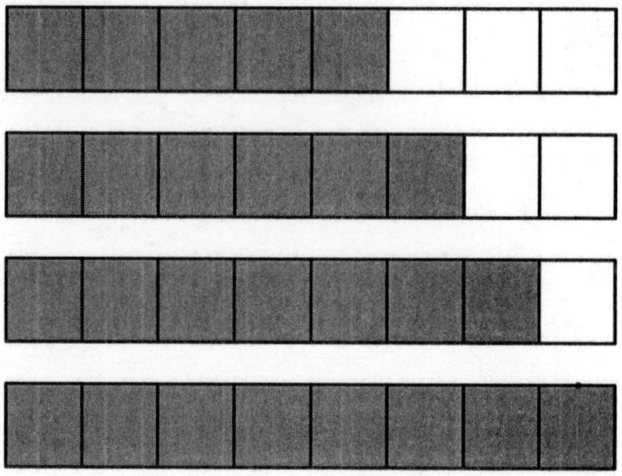

Fourths

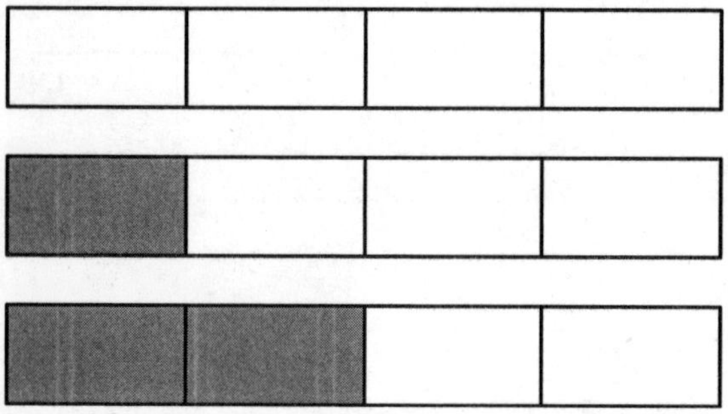

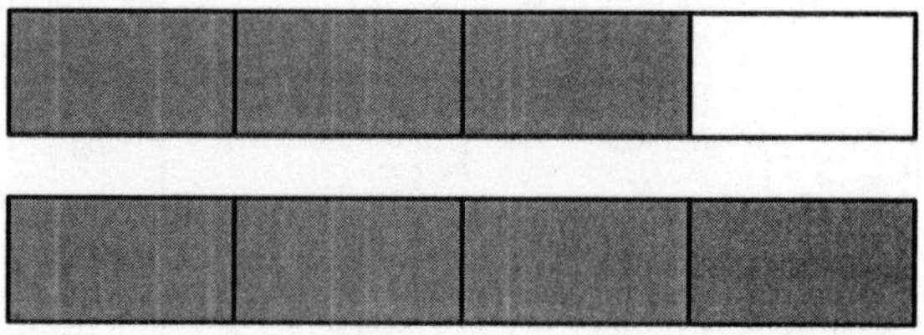

Halves

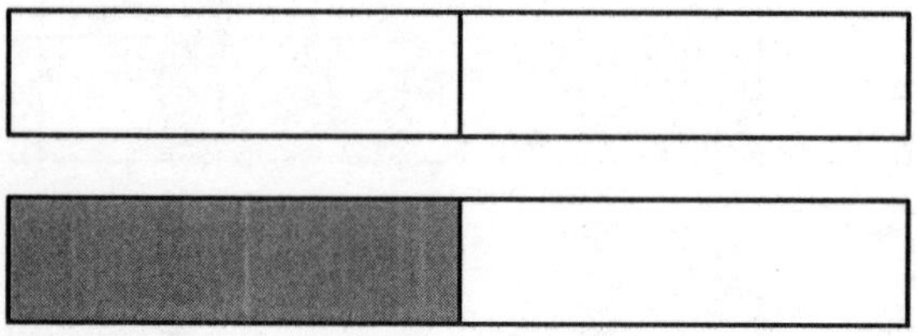

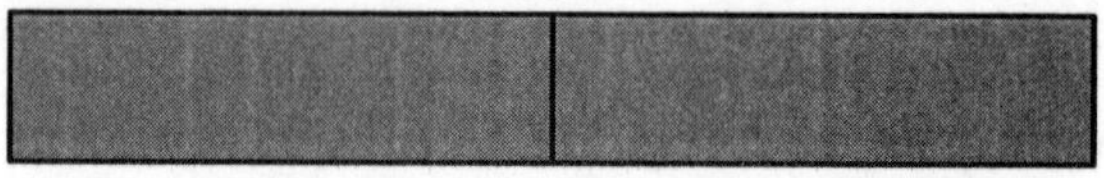

1	2	3	4	5	6	7	8	9	10
11	12	13	14	15	16	17	18	19	20
21	22	23	24	25	26	27	28	29	30
31	32	33	34	35	36	37	38	39	40
41	42	43	44	45	46	47	48	49	50
51	52	53	54	55	56	57	58	59	60
61	62	63	64	65	66	67	68	69	70
71	72	73	74	75	76	77	78	79	80
81	82	83	84	85	86	87	88	89	90
91	92	93	94	95	96	97	98	99	100

Nine Patch

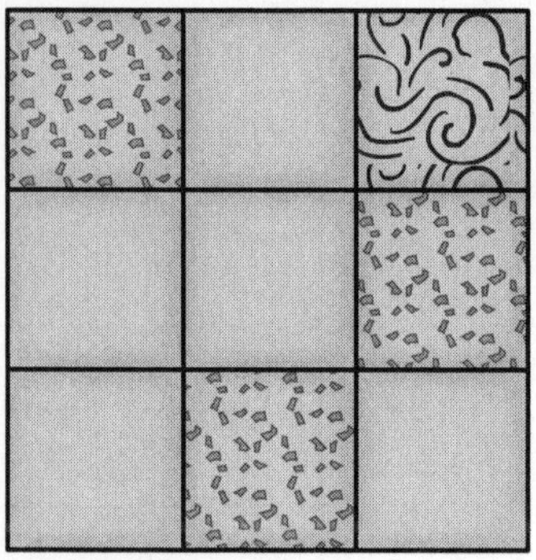

The Open Box

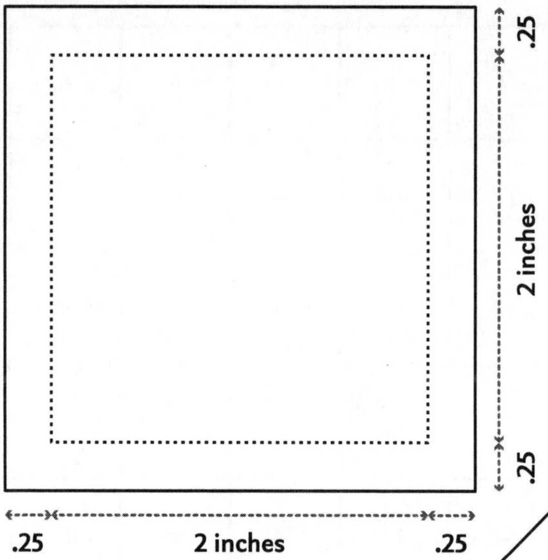

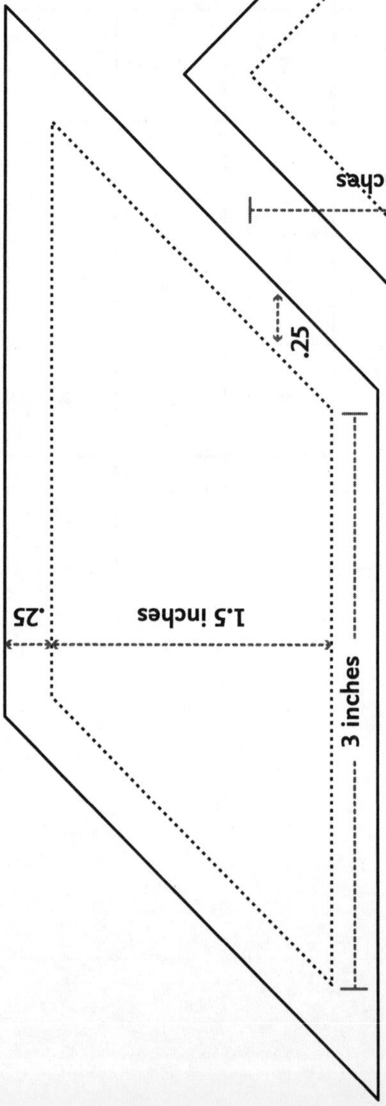

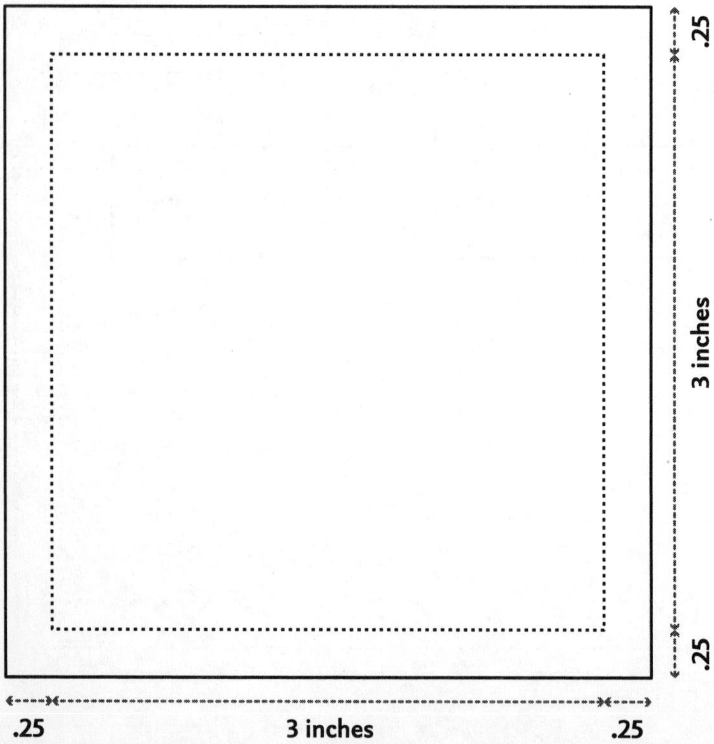

.25

2 inches

.25

.25   2 inches   .25

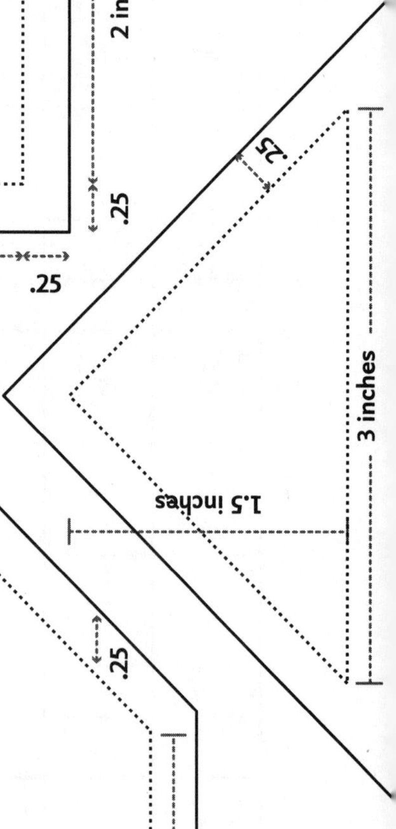

.25

.25

3 inches

.25

3 inches

.25

.25

.25   3 inches   .25

1.5 inches

1.5 inches

.25

.25

3 inches

3 inches

1.5 inches

Roman Square

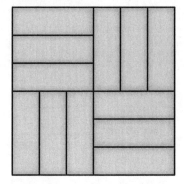

Pinwheel

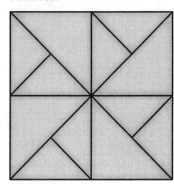

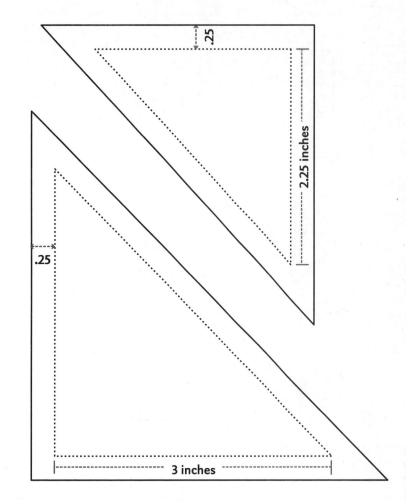

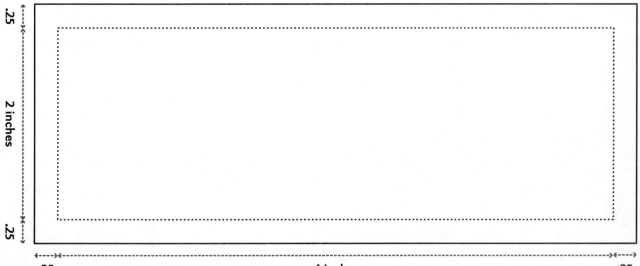

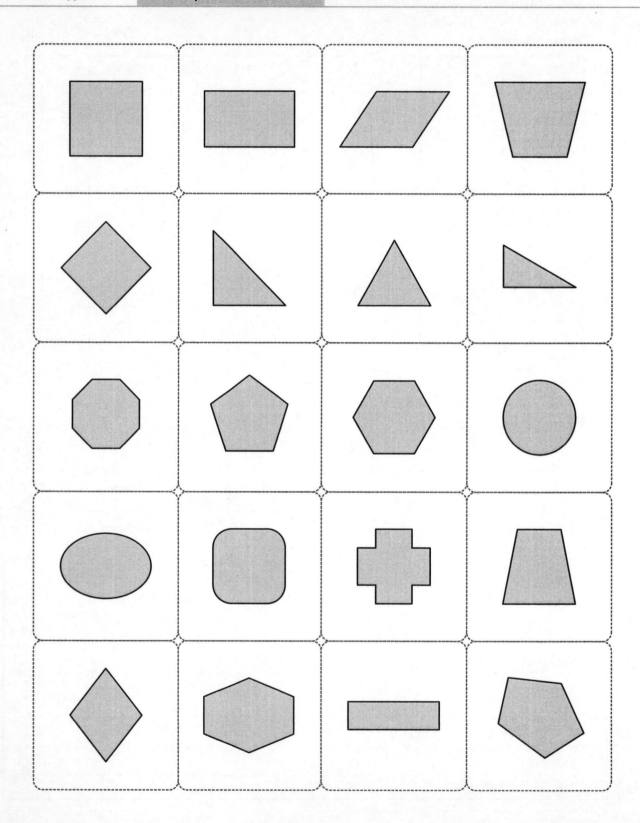

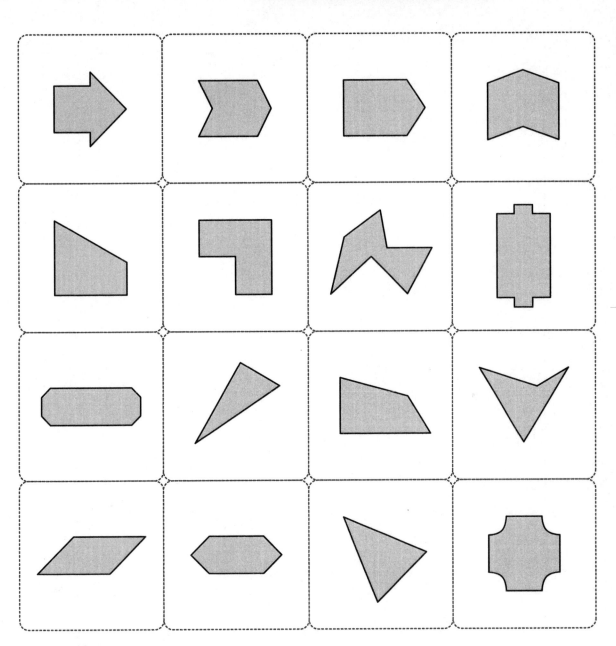

Possible Properties List

Number of Sides	Similar Shapes	Quadrilateral
Equal Sides	Right Angle	Pentagon
Parallel Sides	Obtuse Angle	Hexagon
Perpendicular Sides	Acute Angle	Octagon
Length of Sides	Symmetrical	
Congruent Shapes	Number of Vertices	

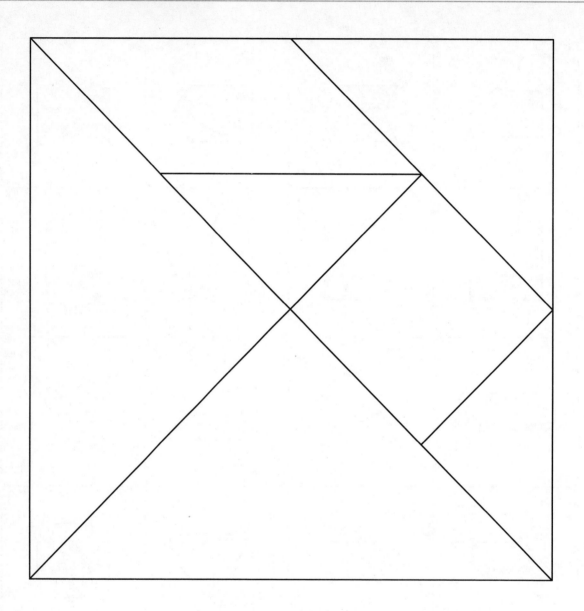

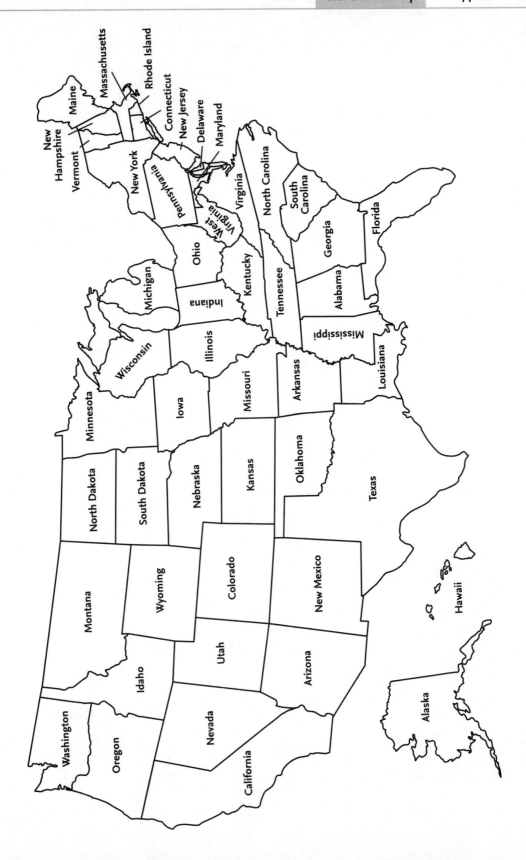

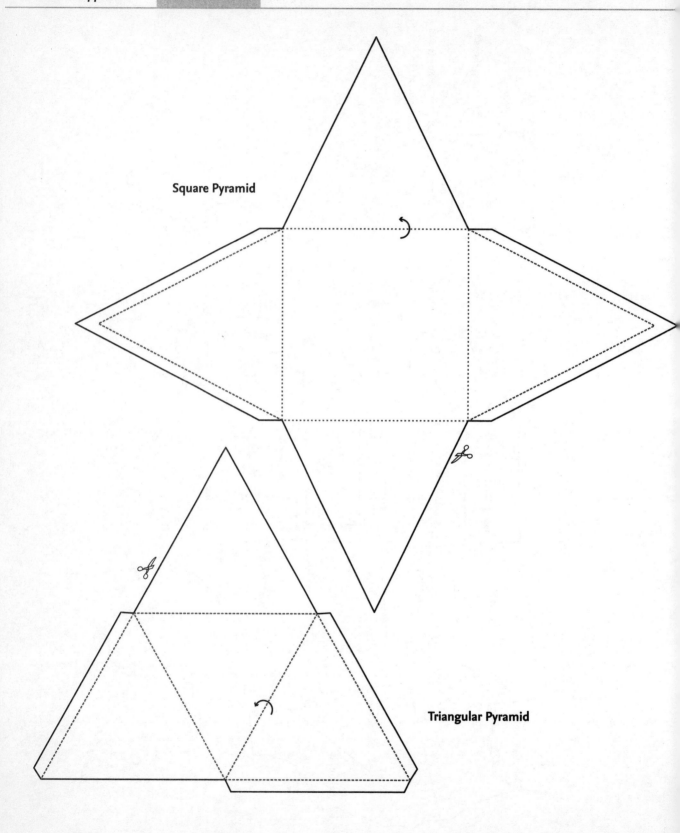

Square Pyramid

Triangular Pyramid

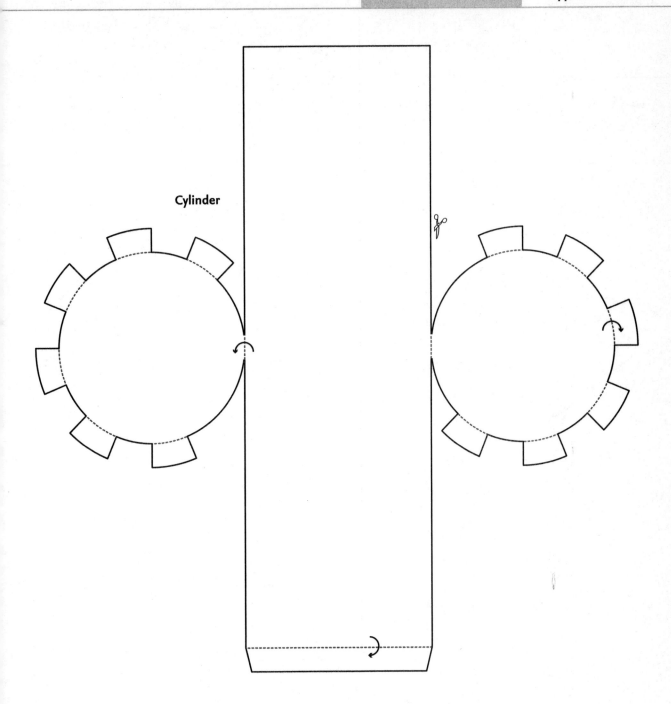

Cylinder

Cone

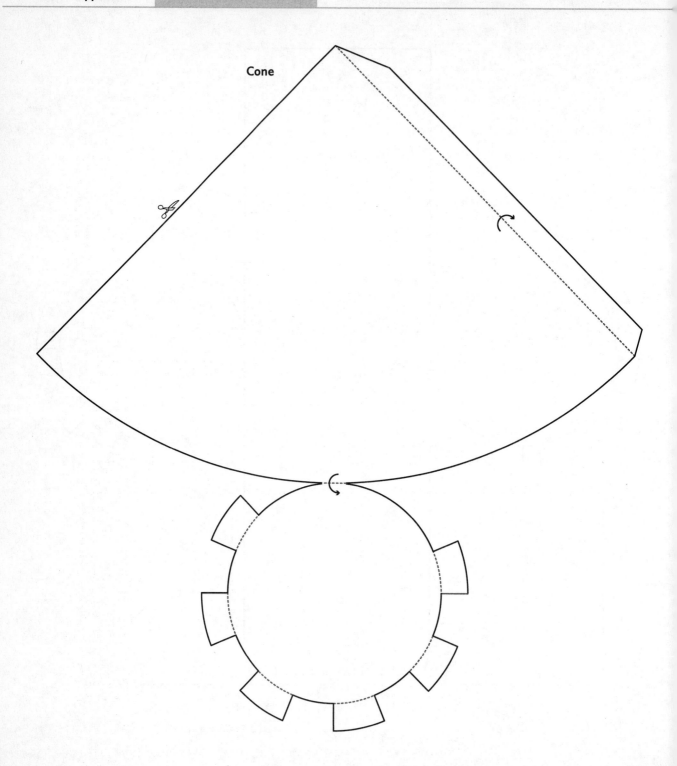

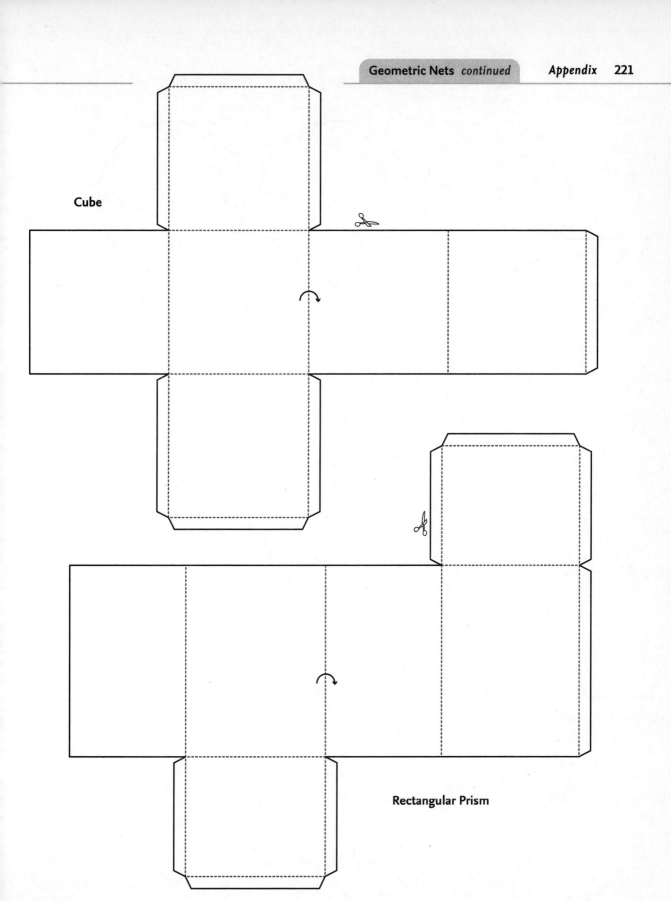

Cube

Rectangular Prism

Large Spinner Pattern

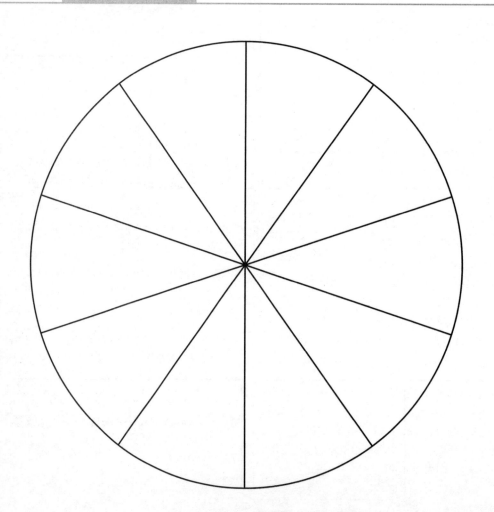

Glossary

A

acute angle: An angle with a measure less than that of a right angle.

addend: A number added. For example, in 5 + 4 = 9, 5 and 4 are addends.

angle: A figure that can be used to show a turn; a corner.

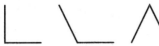

area: A measure in square units of how much surface is covered by a figure.

array: An arrangement of objects, pictures, or numbers in columns and rows.

associative property: When the grouping of addends or factors is changed, the sum or product remains the same. For example:

$(2 + 4) + 6 = 12; 2 + (4 + 6) = 12$

$(1 \times 2) \times 5 = 10; 1 \times (2 \times 5) = 10$

average: The number found by dividing the sum of a group of numbers by the number of addends. For example, $6 + 9 + 8 + 1 = 24$ and $24 \div 4 = 6$, and so 6 is the average. This is *also called* the **mean**.

B

bar graph: A graph in which information is shown by means of rectangular bars.

C

capacity: The amount a container can hold.

Celsius (C): The metric temperature scale. This is *also called* centigrade.

centigrade: *See* **Celsius**.

centimeter (cm): A metric unit used to measure length. 100 cm = 1 meter (m).

circle: A closed figure in which every point is the same distance from a given point, called the center of the circle.

circle graph: A graph that shows information as parts of a circle. This is *also called* a pie graph.

common factor: A number that is a factor of two or more numbers. For example, common factors of 18 and 24 are 1, 2, 3, and 6.

common multiple: A number that is a multiple of two or more numbers. For example, common multiples of 2 and 3 are 6, 12, 18, 24, and 30.

commutative property: When the order of addends or factors is changed, the sum or product remains the same. For example:

$6 + 7 = 13$ and $7 + 6 = 13$; $9 \times 6 = 54$ and $6 \times 9 = 54$

composite numbers: An integer that can be divided by other whole numbers besides 1 and itself. For example, 24 is composite because it can be divided by itself, 1, 2, 3, 4, 6, and 8.

cone: A three-dimensional solid that has a circular base.

congruent figures: Figures that are the same size and shape.

coordinate pairs: An ordered pair of numbers that locates a point on a coordinate plane or grid. The first number denotes the position on the x-axis, and the second number denotes the position on the y-axis. For a pair, go right for the first number, then up from 0 for the second number.

cube: A three-dimensional solid that has six square faces of equal size.

cylinder: A three-dimensional solid with two circular faces that are congruent and a surface connecting the two faces.

D

data: Facts or information.

decimal: A number with one or more digits to the right of the decimal point. For example, 1.4, 2.03, and 0.569 are decimals.

denominator: The number written below the bar in a fraction.

diagonal: A line segment that extends between two vertices or corners that are not next to each other in a polygon.

diameter: A line segment that goes from one side of a circle to the other and passes through the center.

difference: The answer to a subtraction problem. For example, 5 is the difference in $12 - 7 = 5$.

digit: Any one of the following 10 symbols: 0, 1, 2, 3, 4, 5, 6, 7, 8, and 9.

dimension: A measurement of height, width, or length.

distributive property: A number outside the parenthesis is distributed to those inside the parenthesis. The results are the same whether the operation inside the parenthesis is done first and then the answer is multiplied or if each number inside is multiplied separately and the operation inside the parenthesis is applied last. For example, $6(3 + 9)$ can be figured $6 \times 12 = 72$ or $(6 \times 3) + (6 \times 9) = 18 + 54 = 72$.

dividend: The number that is divided in a division problem.

divisor: The number by which a number is being divided. For example, in $6 \div 3 = 2$, the divisor is 3.

E

endpoint: The point at either end of a line segment. It is the beginning point of a ray.

equation: A mathematical sentence with an equal sign. For example, $6 + 9 = 15$ and $(4 \times 3) + 6 = 18$ are both equations.

equilateral triangle: A triangle that has three congruent sides.

equivalent fractions: Fractions that are made of different numbers but represent the same amount or value. For example, ½ and ²⁄₄ are equivalent fractions.

estimate: A number that tells about how much or how many. It is close to the exact number.

even number: A whole number that is a multiple of two. All numbers that have a 0, 2, 4, 6, or 8 in the ones place are even. For example, 72 and 3,456 are even numbers.

F

face: A flat surface of a three-dimensional solid.

factor: One of two or more numbers that are multiplied to give a product. For example, in $5 \times 6 = 30$, 5 and 6 are factors of 30.

Fahrenheit (F): The English temperature scale.

flip: A move that makes a figure face in the opposite direction.

fraction: A number that names a part of a whole, a part of a collection, or a part of a region. For example, ½, ³⁄₈, and ¹⁵⁄₁₆ are fractions.

fraction greater than one: A fraction whose numerator is larger than its denominator and represents more than one whole. For example, ⁸⁄₆ and ⁹⁄₄ are fractions greater than one. This is *also called* an improper fraction.

G

gram (g): A metric measure of mass (weight).

H

hemisphere: A three-dimensional solid figure that is shaped like half of a round ball.

hexagon: A closed figure made up of six line segments.

horizontal: A line segment that is parallel to the horizon.

I

identity property: In addition, the number resulting in the identity property is 0. Adding 0 to any number equals the same number. In multiplication, the number resulting in the identity property is 1. Multiplying any number by 1 equals the same number. For example, $35 + 0 = 35$ and $43 \times 1 = 43$.

improper fraction: *See* **fraction greater than one**.

inequality: A sentence that contains < (less than) or > (greater than).

integers: The set of positive whole numbers, their opposites (negative numbers), and 0. For example, −3, −2, −1, 0, +1, +2, and +3 are integers.

intersecting lines: Lines that meet or cross at a common point.

isosceles triangle: A triangle that has two congruent lines.

K

kilogram (kg): A metric measurement for mass (weight) equal to 1,000 grams. It is approximately 2.2 pounds.

kilometer (km): A metric measurement for distance equal to 1,000 meters. It is approximately five-eighths of a mile.

L

like denominators: Denominators in two or more fractions that are alike. For example, ⁷⁄₁₆ and ³⁄₁₆ have like denominators.

line: A straight path that goes on without end in either direction.

line graph: A graph that uses a broken line to show changes in data over time.

line of symmetry: The line along which a figure can be folded so that the two halves match exactly.

line plot: A diagram that organizes information using a number line.

line segment: Part of a line. A line segment has two endpoints.

liter (l): A metric measure for capacity. A liter is slightly larger than a quart.

M

mean: The number found by adding together a group of numbers and dividing the sum by the number of addends. This is *also called* the **average**.

median: The middle number when a group of numbers is arranged from least to greatest. In the group of numbers (3, 5, 7, 8, 11), 7 is the median because it is in the center. If the set of numbers is an even amount, for example, (2, 5, 7, 10), the median is the average of the two center numbers (5 + 7 ÷ 2 = 6). In this example, 6 is the median.

meter (m): A metric measure for length. A meter is slightly over 39 inches.

milliliter (mL): A metric measure for capacity. 1,000 milliliters = 1 liter.

mixed number: A number composed of a whole number and a fraction. For example, 2 ¾ is a mixed number.

mode: The number or numbers that are found most often in a set of numbers. For example, in (2, 3, 3, 4, 5, 3, 8, 7, 4, 3), 3 is the mode.

multiple: A product of two numbers. For example, in 2 × 4 = 8, 8 is a multiple of 2 and 4.

N

negative number: A number that is less than zero. For example, −4, −10, and −25 are negative numbers.

net: A flat pattern that can be folded to make a solid.

number line: A straight line that is used to show the relative order of numbers, both positive and negative.

numerator: The number written above the bar in a fraction.

O

obtuse angle: An angle greater than that of a right angle but smaller than 180 degrees.

octagon: A closed figure made up of eight line segments.

odd number: A whole number that is not a multiple of 2. If the ones digit is a 1, 3, 5, 7, or 9, the number is odd. For example, 49 and 4,621 are odd numbers.

ordered pairs: A pair of numbers in which the first number is to be considered first and the other number second.

outcome: A result in a probability exercise.

P

parallel lines: Lines in the same plane that are always the same distance apart. They will never intersect.

parallelogram: A four-sided shape in which both pairs of opposite sides are parallel.

pentagon: A closed figure made up of five line segments.

perimeter: The distance around a figure.

perpendicular lines: Two lines or line segments that cross or meet to form right angles.

pictograph: A graph that uses pictured objects to convey ideas and information.

pie graph: *See* **circle graph.**

place value: The value assigned to each place in a numeral, depending upon its base. For example, in base 10, the first place has a value of 1, the second place 10, the third place 100, and so forth.

point: An exact place or position in space, represented by a dot.

polygon: A closed figure made up of line segments with three or more sides.

positive numbers: Numbers that are greater than zero.

prime numbers: A whole number that has only itself and 1 as factors. For example, 11, 13, and 17 are prime numbers.

prism: A three-dimensional solid whose ends are parallel, shaped as one of several polygons, and whose sides are parallelograms.

probability: The chance that an event will occur.

product: The answer to a multiplication problem. For example, in 5 × 3 = 15, 15 is the product.

pyramid: A three-dimensional solid whose base can be any polygon and whose faces are triangles.

Q

quadrilateral: A polygon with four sides.

quotient: The answer to a division problem. For example, in 36 ÷ 4 = 9, 9 is the quotient.

R

radius: A line segment that connects the center of a circle to any point on the circle.

range: The difference between the greatest and least numbers in a set of data.

ray: A line segment extending from one endpoint that goes on forever in the other direction.

rectangle: A four-sided figure whose opposite sides are parallel and have four right angles.

rectangular prism: A three-dimensional solid with six faces that are rectangles.

rectangular pyramid: A three-dimensional solid whose base is a rectangle and whose faces are triangles.

remainder: The number that is left over after one whole number is divided by another.

rhombus: A parallelogram with all sides the same length.

right angle: An angle of 90 degrees.

right triangle: A triangle that has one right angle.

rounding: Showing how many or how much of a quantity by expressing the number to the nearest ten, hundred, thousand, and so on.

S

scalene triangle: A triangle with all three sides having different lengths.

similar figures: Figures having the same shape, but not the same size.

simplest form of a fraction: A fraction whose numerator and denominator can only be reduced by 1 and itself. For example, ¾ is in simplest form; 6/8 is not.

slide: A motion in which every point of a figure moves the same distance in the same direction.

sphere: A three-dimensional figure that is shaped like a round ball.

square: A two-dimensional shape having four sides the same length and four right angles.

sum: The answer to an addition problem. For example, in 5 + 4 = 9, 9 is the sum.

T

trapezoid: A two-dimensional figure having four sides but only one set of parallel sides.

tree diagram: A diagram that shows different combinations of outcomes for a particular event.

triangle: *See* **equilateral triangle, isosceles triangle, right triangle**, and **scalene triangle**.

triangular prism: A prism whose bases are triangles.

triangular pyramid: A pyramid whose base is a triangle.

turn: A motion of a figure in which it rotates around a single point.

U

unlike denominators: Denominators in two or more fractions that are different. For example, ⅔ and 5/6 have unlike denominators.

V

vertex (vertices): A point common to two sides on an angle or triangle or three edges of a prism.

vertical: A line segment that goes up and down.

volume: The number of cubic units that can be found inside a container.

W

weight: The measure of how heavy something is.

whole number: Any of the numbers 0, 1, 2, 3, 4, 5, and so on.

X

x-axis: The horizontal number line in a coordinate system.

Y

y-axis: The vertical number line in a coordinate system.

Bibliography

Baratta-Lorton, Mary. *Mathematics Their Way*. Menlo Park, CA: Innovative Learning Publications, 1995.

Burk, Donna, Allyn Snider, and Paula Symonds. *Box It or Bag It Mathematics*. Salem, OR: The Math Learning Center, 1988.

Candler, Laura. *Discovering Decimals*. San Clemente, CA: Kagan Publishing, 1997.

Franco, Betsy, Christine Losq, Jane McCabe, and Jill Troy. *Understanding Geometry, Level B*. Wilmington, MA: Houghton Mifflin, 1998.

Head, Debby, Libby Pollett, and Michael J. Arcidiacono. *Opening Eyes to Mathematics 3–4*. Salem, OR: The Math Learning Center, 1995.

Hoogeboom, Shirley, and Judy Goodnow. *The Problem Solver 4*. Alpharetta, GA: Creative Publications, 1987.

Jones, Graham A., and Carol A. Thornton. *Data, Chance & Probability: Grades 4–6 Activity Book*. Vernon Hills, IL: Learning Resources, Inc., 1993.

Principles and Standards for School Mathematics. Reston, VA: National Council of Teachers of Mathematics, 2000.

Schiro, Michael. *Mega-Fun Math Games*. New York: Scholastic Inc., 1995.

Strategies for Instruction in Mathematics. Raleigh, NC: State Board of Education North Carolina Department of Public Instruction, 1993.

The Super Source for Tangrams. White Plains, NY: Cuisenaire Company of America, Inc., 1996.

Index